PROLETARIAN LEADERSHIP IN POWER: WHAT WE CAN LEARN FROM LENIN, CASTRO, AND THE FSLN

By Mary-Alice Waters

I0805395

"Politics begin where millions of men and women are," Lenin told the Extraordinary Congress of the Russian Communist Party in March, 1918, "where there are not thousands, but millions, that is where serious politics begin."

And that understanding was what guided the Bolsheviks during the tumultuous years of the Russian revolution and its early struggle for survival.

Proletarian revolutions occur when the great masses of men and women march onto the stage of history and take command of their own destinies. At such times the oppressed and exploited classes move with overwhelming power and speed, learning in a few days the political lessons that in nonrevolutionary times might take decades to be absorbed as part of the collective consciousness of the working class.

The test of proletarian leadership is not simply its capacity to see the way forward. Even more decisive is its ability to learn from and move with the working masses at those decisive moments in history when their courage and determination inevitably surpass the projections of even the best of leaderships. The ultimate test is whether the organized vanguard will be as bold and resolute as the millions-strong who are fighting with unparalleled tenacity because they see a glimmer of hope, a possibility of building society on new foundations once the brutal, inhuman social relations of the existing order have been destroyed.

A little over a year ago in Nicaragua we saw an example of such a revolutionary explosion, led by a vanguard that proved itself worthy of the workers and peasants who looked to it for leadership.

After twenty years of struggle, a heroic mass insurrection brought down one of the most hated dictatorships in Latin America, the Somoza dynasty, "Made in the U.S.A."

As Fidel Castro explained in Managua on July 19 of this year, when he spoke to the half million people gathered to celebrate the first anniversary of that revolutionary victory, the FSLN, the Sandinista National Liberation Front, proved itself to be the vanguard, "not because they want to give themselves the title of vanguard, but because they learned how to win for themselves the place of vanguard in the history and in the struggle of their people."

They proved their capacity to persevere against great odds, to learn from the initiatives and determination of the Nicaraguan people and to lead their struggle forward.

That victory a year ago was our victory. It was a victory for our class, the working class, the world over. And we felt it right here in the United States.

Those of you who were at the convention of the Socialist Workers Party last August will remember what an inspiration it was when Fred Murphy and Pedro Camejo returned from the still embattled city of Managua, coming directly to our convention, to bring us a first hand account. When Camejo began his report with the statement, "Comrades, the socialist revolution in Nicaragua has begun," we all knew that a threshold of history had been crossed. We knew the unfolding struggle in Central America would have profound repercussions for us here in the United States.

The Nicaraguan revolution has been the most important political development in the world during the last year. But that fact does not diminish

This talk was given at the Socialist Educational and Activists Conference in Oberlin, Ohio, August 3, 1980.

the importance of a second revolutionary upheaval that has occurred in the same part of the world.

A few months before the Sandinista victory another stinging blow was dealt to U.S. imperialism. The Gairy dictatorship on the Caribbean island of Grenada was overthrown through an insurrection, and a workers' and farmers' government was established under the leadership of the New Jewel Movement. Like the FSLN, the New Jewel Movement is consciously setting out to follow the Cuban road, to implement social and economic policies that—as our election slogan puts it—place "human needs before profits."

Nicaragua, Grenada, Cuba—the "three giants rising up on the doorstep of imperialism"—have altered the course of world history in the last eighteen months. Nicaragua and Grenada by resolutely setting out to organize and mobilize the working masses of those countries to defend their revolutions and deepen their anti-imperialist, anti-capitalist course. Cuba by mobilizing its people by the millions to reaffirm their proletarian internationalist commitment to stand shoulder to shoulder with their Grenadian, Nicaraguan, Salvadoran, and Guatemalan brothers and sisters against imperialism.

As Fidel put it in his March 8 speech to the Federation of Cuban Women, "one must have a sense of history to know what . . . revolutions mean here, next to the imperialist monster; yes, what the Cuban Revolution and its firm, unwavering line has meant."

We share that sense of history.

We share the assessment of our Cuban, Nicaraguan, Salvadoran, Guatemalan, and Grenadian comrades that as the working masses of the Caribbean and Central America succeed in throwing off the yoke of imperialist domination and becoming their own masters, U.S. imperialism will not sit by with folded hands. It will not watch passively as a second, much less a third or fourth, workers' state is born in a region the Yankee rulers once considered their own private lake.

They are not sitting on folded hands now. They are already intervening economically and militarily to crush the revolutionary struggle in El Salvador, and to roll back the victories already achieved in Nicaragua and Grenada. We cannot predict the time, the place, or the forms of the coming battles. But step by step the confrontation is sharpening throughout the region. It will intensify no matter who is elected president of the United States in November because imperialism has no choice. Every revolutionary advance threatens its survival.

For revolutionists inside the United States, as for our compañeros throughout the Caribbean and Central America, this means being conscious of the stakes involved, of the forces that are in motion.

For us, solidarity with the struggles of our brothers and sisters who are breaking the chains of Yankee imperialism is not only a matter of aiding their struggle and defending them against imperialism. It is an indispensable part of the education and preparation of the American working class to do away with that imperialist monster once and for all. Class-consciousness is impossible without internationalist consciousness, for the simple reason that our class is not national, it is international. And however difficult revolutionary victories may be in other parts of the world, the most difficult of all will be right here in the United States.

Thus we approach every revolutionary victory anywhere in the world with two things in mind: first, how we can organize the American working class to help defend and extend that revolution; and second, what we can learn from it. What can we learn that will improve the chances of a successful revolutionary struggle by our class in this country? What can we learn from those who have proved their capacities as combat leaders of the working class?

Other talks and classes at this educational conference will take up the objective side of the changing relationship of class forces on a world scale, the advances being made by the working people, and the blows being dealt imperialism. I want to concentrate today on the subjective side of the equation, the question of leadership.

The caliber of the revolutionary leadership involved is itself an objective factor that affects our assessment of what is happening.

In the two years of 1959–60 the July 26 Movement came to power in Cuba, established a workers' and farmers' government, mobilized the masses of the Cuban people to break the economic power of the capitalist class and sever the chains of imperialist bondage. That was the first example of the dictatorship of the proletariat in our hemisphere. This was a historic breakthrough. For the first time since the Bolsheviks did it in 1917 a revolution was led by forces that were non-Stalinist in origin. It was a qualitative step forward in resolving the crisis of proletarian leadership on a world scale, *which is the central crisis of humanity.*

Twenty-one years have passed. The Cuban revolution has survived and grown stronger despite Washington's illegal occupation of Guantanamo, its blockade, sabotage, bacteriological warfare, military aggression, assassination attempts, and everything else. Not only has it survived, it has achieved the kinds of advances in the standard of living of the Cuban people that only a nationalized, planned economy can bring.

And it has accomplished something that is historically unprecedented. It has sustained the revolutionary mobilization of the Cuban people for more than two decades. By comparison, powerful objective factors had exhausted the Soviet toiling masses by 1923–4. One really has to have a sense of history to appreciate that, to understand what it means to be able to hold in check those whom Raúl Castro has so aptly christened the "faint hearts," what it means to prevent those who have grown tired of the struggle and see only individual solutions from gaining the upper hand.

Now, with revolutions on the march in Nicaragua and Grenada, led by forces that look to the lessons of the Cuban revolution for guidance, and to the Castroist leadership, the proletarian revolution is being extended in the Americas.

It is safe to say that we ourselves have not yet fully absorbed the meaning of that fact. We are entering a new period in history. We are witnessing the conscious extension of the socialist revolution under proletarian internationalist leadership. Another big step is being taken in resolving the crisis of leadership of the world working class.

Our revolution, *our* current, is expanding. There are today a growing number of revolutionists who, like us, trace their continuity to Marx and Engels and Lenin. Who try, as best as they are able, to absorb and to apply every lesson of the class struggle from 1848 on. And we who are Trotskyists know that those who study, understand, and apply the essential lessons of Marx, Engels, and Lenin will not lose their bearings in the class struggle today. No matter what they call themselves, we will all be travelling the same road together, because Trotskyism to us is nothing but Marxism and Leninism in our time.

In trying to appreciate the caliber of this revolutionary current, I want to focus on the record of the Castro leadership and the Sandinistas in power. We are generally more preoccupied with the problems of the working class taking power than holding it, since in most countries of the world the bourgeoisie remains more or less firmly seated in power. But in truth, that is the relatively easier task. The biggest challenge of "serious politics"—to use Lenin's phrase—is to mobilize and organize the great mass of oppressed and exploited to march forward in the construction of a new social order. To use governmental power to mobilize the collective strength of the workers and peasants and direct it against the onslaught of imperialism and its domestic lackeys. To change social consciousness and lay the foundations of a new economic order. To remain a bulwark of the world revolution and to subordinate all else to that.

For the first time in twenty years profound social revolutions are taking place right here in our hemisphere where we can be part of them, study them step by step, and learn from them. This is crucially important because it expands our own revolutionary experience. It helps us to go beyond the relatively more isolated existence we are forced into by the current conditions of the class struggle in this country. It teaches us to think broadly in basic class terms. How and why do *classes* move? How does a conscious Marxist leadership in power go about changing the course of history?

Fidel posed the issue very well in 1966, in a speech to the Confederation of Cuban Workers. He said, "When one agitates from a barricade, when one issues a revolutionary proclamation, it all looks easy from afar. . . . Yet the most difficult task is the task of creating a new society. The most difficult task is to convert ideas into realities. . . . Stop to think what a revolution is at the outset. . . . It is a struggling, working beehive of men who, though filled with good intentions, lack experience, lack knowledge, lack training. And suddenly, there is thrust on the shoulders of these men the task of making the nation move forward, administering everything. . . .

"And if I were asked what was the principal merit of a generation that undertakes a revolution, my reply would be: having made the revolution and having marched forward despite their great ignorance. . . ."

That is what every revolution is like, and we should be humble enough to recognize that ours will be no different. Certainly the Bolshevik revolution with the best Marxist leadership the working class has known in our century was no different. As Lenin was the first to insist, they made "many foolish mistakes."

In taking a look at the record of the Castro leadership in power, and the record of those who are today setting out to follow the Cuban road, it is useful to take the October revolution and the Bolsheviks under Lenin as our reference point. It is one we share with the Fidelistas who likewise consider that first great proletarian revolution to have been a watershed in the history of humanity.

What is a revolution?

We need to start with two basic questions.

What is a revolution? And what is the essence of revolutionary leadership?

Most of us have never been in a country where a revolution was taking place, much less lived through one. So I want to begin to answer those two questions by making some observations about Nicaragua. I just returned from Managua where I was able to join half a million other Sandinistas for the July 19 celebration of the first anniversary of the mass insurrection that drove Somoza from power.

When you step out of your plane at the Augusto Cesar Sandino airport in Managua, you know that somewhere, up there in the air, you crossed a class line.

The first thing you realize is that you're not scared of the police. Army, militia, police. They're all over the place. But you feel good about it, and so does everybody else. Almost everybody else. The "forces of repression" are all laughing, smiling, joking with the hundreds of ordinary working people milling around.

When you go through immigration formalities and say you're from a socialist publication in the United States that supports the revolution, you get treated with warm hospitality. The NBC-TV crew that was right behind me got a noticeably different reception. The Sandinista officials weren't discourteous but there was no deferential treatment for the arrogant representatives of the imperialist press. They had to stand in line just like everyone else. They considered it an affront, since they thought they were doing the Nicaraguans a favor by being there.

As you leave the airport, you are struck by the devastation. One year after the heavy fighting ended, grass has grown tall and trees have sprouted, but driving through what used to be the tax-free light-industry zone between the airport and downtown Managua, you see factory after factory that is just a bombed out shell.

Banners and posters are everywhere, on fences, walls, and billboards.

"Welcome, comrades from the world over. Welcome to free Nicaragua, land of Sandino."

A huge billboard showing a young woman in fatigues with a gun on her shoulder, saying, "I'm a militia woman."

"To learn to read and write is to strike another blow."

Another billboard, beautifully painted with a wildlife scene, and the slogan, "The trees and the birds and the animals of Nicaragua are our heritage. Let's conserve them."

A banner on a factory fence proclaims: "The women of Nicaragua are present in the fight to reconstruct our country."

And everywhere, the words of Sandino, "Only the workers and peasants will go all the way."

After you've had a chance to walk around a little, and get a feel for the city, two things strike you.

The first is, you feel like you're in a country where the Young Socialist Alliance has just taken power. Young people are in charge of everything—the traffic, the militia, the army, the government ministries, the trade unions, the literacy crusade, directing the huge mobilization of July 19. Moreover, they're all armed and disciplined. One of the leaders of the July 19th Sandinista Youth told us that the median age of the FSLN is twenty-four.

Of course, this is not surprising. It's the same in all revolutions. It's the youth of Nicaragua who fought and died to get rid of Somoza, who gave their lives because they knew that if the FSLN won there would be a future for everybody. A new day would dawn for all of Nicaragua's oppressed and exploited.

Sometimes our class enemies note things that capture the truth. When a number of us were waiting around for our press credentials to be processed at one of the hotels in Managua we got into a discussion with the U.S. Air Force crew that flew Donald McHenry, U.S. ambassador to the United Nations, to Nicaragua for the July 19 celebration. We asked them if they were going to walk around and get a feel for life in revolutionary Managua while they were there. They immediately replied, "No way. We've been instructed to stay off the streets. This is a dangerous place."

When we looked rather puzzled, they went on. "You know, there's kids running around here with guns! They're all over the place! A year ago most of them couldn't even spell the word g-u-n and now every one of 'em's got one!"

Then someone else on the crew chimed in and said, "Yeah, and they're disciplined as hell."

They were looking at things from the other side of the class line, but they certainly captured the essence of what's happened in Managua.

The second thing that strikes you about Nicaragua is that the whole country is smiling. Despite the poverty, the destruction, the enormous problems they face, you can feel that people are alive with happiness. It's as if you walked through Harlem some morning and everybody was smiling. Not only that, but every tenth person had a rifle slung over his or her shoulder, with a gang of kids hanging around, smiling and joking and laughing. You would know something fundamental had changed. That those rifles would be used with grim determination if need be, to protect those newly won smiles.

"Revolutions," Lenin said, "are festivals of the oppressed and exploited."

They are people's revolutions.

"Yes, the *people's* revolution. Social-Democracy has fought, and is quite rightly fighting, against the bourgeois-democratic abuse of the word 'people'. It demands that this word shall not be used to cover up failure to understand class antagonisms within the people. It insists categorically on the need for complete class independence for the party of the proletariat. However, it does not divide the "people" into "classes" so that the advanced class will become locked up within itself . . . it does that so that the advanced class, which does not suffer from the half-heartedness, vacillation, and indecision of the intermediate classes, should fight with all the greater energy and enthusiasm for the cause of the whole people, at the head of the whole people.

"At no other time are the masses of the people in a position to come forward so actively as creators of a new social order, as at a time of revolution. At such times people are capable of performing miracles, if judged by the limited, philistine yardstick of gradualist progress."

The job of revolutionary parties at such times, Lenin said, is to "show them the shortest and most direct route to complete, absolute, and decisive victory. . . . Let the bourgeois opportunists contemplate the future reaction with craven fear. The workers will not be intimidated either by the thought that reaction intends to be terrible, or that the bourgeoisie proposes to recoil." ["Two Tactics of Social-Democracy in the Democratic Revolution" Lenin's *Selected Works*, Vol. 1, pp. 503–504.]

That was written at the beginning of the 1905 revolution in Russia. But it could just as easily have been a description of Nicaragua—or Grenada—in 1980.

Proletarian leadership

When millions of human beings march onto the stage of history, they don't all march in step. First of all, the working class itself is divided and stratified. Young and old, skilled and unskilled, male and female, oppressed nationalities and oppressor nationalities, organized and unorganized, hereditary proletarians (those whose families have been part of the working class and whose children will be) and those who have only recently been forced into the ranks of the proletariat. Those who are working in heavy industry, and those employed in light industry, transport, services. And there are many other divisions and stratifications you can think of, giving rise to different experiences, different levels of consciousness, and different paces of political development. Thus the working class never marches in straight ranks in a revolutionary process.

The other oppressed classes are part of a "people's revolution" too, and they move at a still different rhythm, subject to divergent experiences and class needs. The peasantry or small farmers, the petty-bourgeois producers and shopkeepers.

Mobilizing, educating, organizing the most conscious component of the working class to lead these diverse social layers, to homogenize their understanding and experience, is the very heart of revolutionary politics.

The better the leadership of the revolutionary vanguard has prepared itself for this, the better it understands the laws of history, the more thoroughly it has absorbed that politics is essentially concentrated economics, that politics is the relationship between *classes*—the fewer and the less costly the mistakes will be. But the fundamental dividing line between proletarian revolutionists and petty-bourgeois radicals of all kinds is not pristine programmatic purity on paper. What distinguishes a working-class leadership is its unshakeable confidence in and reliance on the capacity of the working class to understand and measure up to its historic tasks, including the task of winning the decisive layers of the other oppressed classes to its side.

This kind of respect for the working classes permeated the first anniversary celebration of the victory of the Nicaraguan revolution on July 19. And it was mutual. The half million Nicaraguan fighters who gathered in the plaza were there to demonstrate their confidence in the FSLN and their readiness to scale the ramparts of Yankeedom if necessary in order to maintain their newly won independence, guarantee their social progress, and help their compañeros in El Salvador to follow the same road.

Their mutual respect between the masses and their leadership was also expressed in the relationship between Fidel and the Nicaraguan people on July 19. Nicaragua has its own national heroes, especially Sandino and Carlos Fonseca Amador, and its own leaders in the FSLN. But more than any other world leader, Fidel symbolizes the aspirations of the Nicaraguan masses. He represents the Cuban revolution, which stood by the Nicaraguan people in their darkest hours and provided decisive aid at the moment when victory was at last within reach. He stands for the socialist revolution in Cuba that has demonstrated what a determined, united people can accomplish, despite all odds, once they have rid themselves of imperialist domination and capitalist exploitation.

After a tumultuous reception, when Fidel finally began to speak, the silence in the plaza was almost total. Fidel joked about it, he said, "This place is so quiet you could hear a mosquito buzz." The Nicaraguan people had been waiting to welcome Fidel for many years.

But that was only half the picture. The other half was Fidel's deep respect for the Nicaraguan masses. He paid tribute to their heroic sacrifices, to the greatness of human will, striving for justice, freedom, and humanity in the land of Sandino. He reviewed the names of the decisive battles in the liberation struggle, and paid tribute to those who shed their blood and paid with their lives in those hours. In Cuba, he told them, in the final days of the struggle last year, millions of people had anxiously awaited the news of those battles, day by day, hour by hour. And the Nicaraguan masses knew that it was true. They knew Fidel understood what they had accomplished. They knew Fidel had been there, with them in spirit, and that the solidarity and aid of the Cuban people had tipped the balance.

Fidel expressed this deep respect for the Nicaraguan people when he told them, "We come humbly to learn and to be influenced. We are sure that the Sandinista revolution will teach us a great deal."

This genuine mutual respect electrified the rally on July 19. The confidence of the FSLN in the working class, in their capacity and determination to go all the way no matter what the obstacles. And the confidence of the workers and peasants that they had a leadership that understood their determination, a leadership that would not fear to mobilize and use the collective power of the oppressed and exploited, a leadership that, like them, was prepared to go all the way in defense of the interests of the working class.

The attitude of the Nicaraguan people toward their leadership—including its Cuban component—was expressed very well by an eleven-year-old girl who was talking to several members of the SWP in Nicaragua this summer. It was after July 19 and Fidel was still in the country, so the comrades asked her, "What do you think of Fidel?" Her reply, loosely translated, was something like, "Fidel's the greatest."

So the SWP comrades pressed her a little further.

"Why do you think Fidel's the greatest?"

She smiled at them and shot back, "Because Fidel's a Sandinista."

Not a cup of instant coffee

Let's take a look now at the revolutionary process unfolding in Nicaragua, at some of the problems the working class faces as it fights to keep power in its hands and deepen the revolution.

The goal toward which the FSLN-led workers' and farmers' government is moving is the consolidation of a workers' state in Nicaragua—the nationalization and collectivization of the remaining centers of capitalist economic power. That sounds simple enough. But as Maurice Bishop, the prime minister of Grenada, so aptly explained in the interview he gave to *Intercontinental Press* a few weeks ago—a revolution is not like instant coffee. You don't "just throw it in a cup and it comes out presto."

A revolution is a profound transformation of every aspect of social and economic life. It is the restructuring of society from top to bottom. The restructuring of relationships between classes. The beginning of the *elimination* of classes.

You have to stop and think what that means in terms of social relations, what a revolution in consciousness must occur for the exploited class to become the ruling class, and then begin to eliminate itself! That process of restructuring all social relations can only proceed as fast as the material conditions of life are changed not for a few, not for a handful, but for millions.

Classes and their complex interrelationships can't be dissolved like instant coffee, either.

In the early years of the Russian revolution, Lenin explained over and over that getting rid of what he called the "front ranks" of the exploiting class, the landlords and the big industrialists, was no big deal. "In regard to them, the work of destruction is fairly easy; it can be completed within a few months, and sometimes even a few weeks or days."

That's important. It is the first, indispensable step toward settling the question of power; what class holds the political and economic reins of power. But that's just the beginning. It is destroying part of the old. All the classes that exist in capitalist society continue to exist. The political framework of the economic and social relations between them has been altered, but the starting point of revolutionary strategy remains the problem of *class* relations and conflicting *class* interests.

First, the divisions and stratifications within the working class itself remain. How can they be overcome? How do you educate the working class, raise the political and cultural level? How does this new ruling class become fully conscious of its historic class role? How does it really begin ruling?

Second, the new ruling working class must establish harmonious relations with the peasantry or small farmers, and the small producers. They are not proletarians.

In many countries, especially in the countries that have been dominated by imperialism for so many decades, the peasantry constitutes a majority of the population. The proletarian revolution does not expropriate them; in fact, it usually gives them their own private property, their land, for the first time in history. The small producers have different class interests than the workers. But if it is to survive, the proletarian revolution must win and hold their support at the same time that it creates the material conditions that will lead to the withering away of this class.

Third, once you expropriate the sixty families, or the one hundred families, or the one dynasty, and nationalize the basic industries and financial institutions, you still have a lot of big capitalists left. Not just the petty producers. In addition, depending on the size of the economy, there are hundreds of thousands, even millions, of technicians, administrators, engineers, and others who identify their interests with those of the capitalist class. Their knowledge and experience in managing vast capitalist enterprises are indispensable to the working class. Only idiots and infantile ultralefts would propose that all enterprises that exploit human labor be expropriated as soon as the working class seizes power. The only thing that would accomplish would be total economic collapse, bringing suffering and misery to millions.

A fundamental problem of class relations is posed as soon as the political power of the bourgeoisie has been smashed. Within the framework of a death struggle between two irreconcilably hostile classes, how do you get the administrators and technicians, and even some of the bourgeoisie, to work for the proletariat? They have forced us to work for them for centuries. How do we make some of them work for us for a few years in order to minimize the social and economic dislocation of the transition to a nationalized economy planned in the interests of the majority? That is one of the tasks of the revolution. And it's no small matter.

Stop and think about it. Those sitting in this room are the indispensable core of the cadres who are going to help lead the process by which the U.S. working class will expropriate the key industries and financial institutions, and learn how to manage and plan the vast economy of the United States. The day after the U.S. working class comes to power, your primary responsibility will be to make sure that 250 million people can eat every day, stay warm, get to work and back, and do all the other things that are essential to the health and welfare of the vast majority.

Would you know what to do? Would you know where to begin?

Before the workers triumph we'll get a few more years of experience in dealing with things like the two party system, the Douglas Frasers, Andrew Youngs, and Eleanor Smeals, the KKK and the fascists. We will be more confident, more flexible, tougher revolutionary politicians. But running the economy? That's another matter.

Yet that is the task facing our compañeros in Nicaragua and Grenada today. And, except in what they've already accomplished, what they've already proved about their capacities, they are a lot like us. Until a year ago, they were revolutionary politicians and soldiers, not economists and administrators. But on March 14 and July 20, that all changed.

Lenin explained the challenge facing the Bolsheviks on this score in the early years of the Russian revolution.

"When we rap the exploiters' knuckles, render them innocuous, overpower them, it is only half the job," he said. In fact, "it is less than one fourth" the job. "We must make these hands work for us."

"The idea of building communist society exclusively with the hands of the Communists is childish, absolutely childish," he told the Eleventh Congress of the Russian Communist Party in 1922. "We Communists are but a drop in the ocean of people." We may understand politics and history, but will we be able to supply the peasants with goods in exchange for their grain? If we can't "the peasants will say: 'You are splendid fellows; you defended our country. That is why we obeyed you. But if you cannot run the show, get out!' Yes, that is what the peasants will say.

"We Communists shall be able to direct our economy if we succeed in utilising the hands of the bourgeoisie in building up this economy of ours and in the meantime learn from these bourgeoisie and guide them along the road we want them to travel. But when a Communist imagines that he knows everything, when he says: 'I am a responsible Communist, I have beaten enemies far more formidable than any salesman. We have fought at the front and have beaten far more formidable enemies'—it is this prevailing mood that is doing us great harm." ["Eleventh Congress of the R.C.P. (B.)," Lenin's *Selected Works*, Vol. 3, pp. 697–698.]

Class struggle in Nicaragua

How does this relate to what is happening in Nicaragua?

First and foremost, in Nicaragua the question of political power has been settled. A workers' and peasants' government, dominated by the FSLN, was established in the weeks immediately following the mass insurrection that definitively smashed the state structure controlled by Somoza. All land and other economic interests controlled by Somoza and his cohorts were expropriated. Other measures were taken to establish state control over banking, foreign trade, and the prices of basic consumer necessities. The government has used its power to systematically organize and mobilize the masses of workers and poor peasants as its class base, to implement economic and social policies in the interest of the oppressed and exploited. That process has progressively eroded the economic power of the bourgeoisie.

The laws of capitalist accumulation continue to govern in decisive sectors of the economy. The prerogatives of profit and private ownership of major sectors vital to social production continually come into contradiction with government economic planning and decisions on the redistribution of social wealth. The bourgeoisie provides ever-present possibilities for imperialist pressure and blackmail, destabilization, and sabotage. Eventually the remaining capitalist property will have to be taken over. In assessing the direction of motion, in determining whose interests will be served as the existing social and economic contradictions are resolved, the decisive question is: What side of the class line is the government on today? Will its power be used in defense of the working peoples' interests?

The record of the FSLN government offers an unambiguous answer. For one year it has been on a forced march to organize, mobilize, and arm the masses of the workers and peasants, youth, and women to carry through and defend the social gains of the revolution. This process was initiated within weeks of the overthrow of Somoza. Plans for implementing the agrarian reform, literacy crusade, public health measures, neighborhood defense committees, and other programs were begun well before the July 19 victory. The speed with which these campaigns were launched is an indication that the Nicaraguan vanguard is trying to build on the lessons of the Cuban revolution.

The mass mobilization and organization of the Nicaraguan workers and peasants is the guarantee—and the only guarantee—of which class interests the government will defend when it moves to resolve the conflicts and contradictions that are engendered by the remaining capitalist economic relations.

But the question of political power is just the first, not the last issue to be dealt with. In considering some of the economic problems posed, it is worth thinking about some of the parallels between Russia in 1918–22 and Nicaragua today.

As the Bolsheviks repeatedly emphasized, everything they did was conditioned by the fact that they were obliged to start from an utterly ruined economic base and a backward one at that. In a speech to the Russian Communist Youth League in 1922, for example, Trotsky pointed out that before the proletariat proved capable of taking over the productive forces that had been brought to their highest level of development by capitalism, the bourgeoisie, "in the frenzied spasm of the world war" literally annihilated a great part of the material values created by labor from the beginning of primitive capitalist accumulation onward. And that was the foundation on which they were compelled to establish a workers' state.

The destruction in Nicaragua was not so complete as it was in Russia. But some similar problems are posed, and it is in that framework that the FSLN deliberately decided not to immediately nationalize much of the light industry and many large land holdings—so long as their owners get their property producing again. Any property not put into production is subject to immediate expropriation.

In this way they hope to maximize international aid and trade and take advantage of the technical and managerial skills of the capitalists to get industry relaunched after the devastation of the last months of the civil war. At the same time capitalist production takes place in the political framework established by the FSLN government: the welfare of the people rather than profits must come first. To the capitalists they say, "If you want to produce under these rules fine. If you don't, get out. We will not let you stand in the way."

In Nicaragua the Superior Council on Private Enterprise (COSEP), the main organization and voice of the bourgeoisie, took advantage of the foreign press being present for the July 19 celebration. They called a press conference to explain how they look at things.

Their line is very simple. Their spokesmen—with smirks so broad they could hardly talk—said: we are all for the Junta of National Reconstruction. We are all for its economic policies. We think the land reform is just wonderful. Everyone has a right to own land. Of course, the government shouldn't take over any more land from big proprietors. The National Agrarian Reform Institute has plenty. They can divide it up among the peasants and make them happy, so we're against the new law announced on July 19 (which will take idle land away from big owners).

"We recognize that we are a minority." A big step forward in consciousness! "And we are not politicians, we're just businessmen. We don't want to run this country. But a principle is being violated. The people have the right to change their government when they want, and therefore we demand elections."

"From "a minority" to "the people" is an easy transition—verbally.

The COSEP representatives are rightly concerned—from their class point of view—with the question of governmental power. The one thing they know for sure is that it is not now in their hands.

This preoccupation with the question of which class controls state power bothered COSEP's forefathers in Russia in the early 1920s, too. The Bolsheviks were likewise making considerable concessions to domestic and international capitalism during the period of the New Economic Policy. Many ultraleft critics, inside and outside the Communist International, considered such concessions impermissible class collaboration.

Trotsky explained the ABCs of state power. When the bourgeoisie holds state power, he said, it "makes concessions to the working class: universal suffrage, social and factory legislation, national insurance, the shortening of the working day. The bourgeoisie makes a retreat step by step; where necessary it grants a reform; when possible it puts on the pressure again and then makes a retreat. Why? It is manoeuvring; the ruling class is fighting for its rule, for the exploitation of the other class. Of course the reformists suppose that bit by bit they will remake the bourgeois system into a socialist one. And we reply to this: rubbish!—while power is in the hands of the bourgeoisie they will measure out each reform but they know up to what point they can grant a reform. And just for this purpose they have the power in their hands.

"The same inter-relation between state power and reform exists with us too but with just that tiny difference that here the working class is in power and it likewise makes concessions to the bourgeoisie: trading concessions, free trade, the right to profit and the right to carry its bourgeois soul and its bourgeois body through the streets of Moscow with impunity. This considerable concession has been granted but it has been granted by the ruling working class which holds the debit and credit book of its state and which says: 'To this line here I will make a concession but not any further.'"

This is the dilemma of the capitalists in Nicaragua today. And they know it very well. As long as state power is being wielded to defend the needs and interests of the majority, not the private profits of a minority, capitalist enterprise is encircled and living on borrowed time.

The workers' and farmers' government is correct to try to buy time, to make concessions, if need be, to get production going, to entice the bourgeoisie to work. That is in the interests of the workers and peasants today as long as power and decisions on economic and social priorities are firmly in the hands of the workers and peasants. The class struggle has not been superseded; it is occurring in a new framework. The death struggle between irreconcilably hostile classes continues. But for once the workers are maneuvering from a position of strength with a government and army and police behind them. They can all the better afford to make each step forward a defensive move to counter the sabotage of the minority which does not like the new limits set on its privileges.

As long as significant elements of private ownership exist, of course, capitalist relations will be constantly reproduced. So the new framework entails risks and dangers. But—without major imperialist military intervention—it is now too late to reverse the direction of development toward the consolidation of a workers' state.

Such imperialist intervention remains the major threat to the Nicaraguan revolution today. And the FSLN is supremely conscious of the fact that the Nicaraguan bourgeoisie is part of an international class that protects its own. By themselves the Nicaraguan capitalists are today relatively weak, but imperialism is not standing idly by. The bloody civil war raging in El Salvador is part of the international capitalist intervention aimed at eventually rolling back the Nicaraguan revolution. And just as imperialist military action forced the Bolsheviks to move faster than they wanted to on nationalizations, faster than was necessary or desirable given the state of the economy and the level of organization of the working class, imperialist economic and military intervention may well force the FSLN to move faster than would otherwise be necessary or desirable.

The working class and the peasantry

Let's go on to the second big question of class relations, those between the working class and the peasantry. Here expropriation is not an issue. Just the opposite. The workers' and farmers' government must make it easier for this class of small property owners to produce. It must rapidly improve the conditions of life for the peasantry, and over time prove the superiority of collectivization and large-scale mechanized agricultural methods.

It was on this question that the Russian revolution almost floundered—given the devastation, economic dislocation, and famine resulting from the years of imperialist war, invasion, and civil war. The majority of the poor peasants supported the Bolsheviks because the October revolution gave them land and the White armies wanted to take it back for the landlords. But that support was not unlimited. It depended on getting the economy on its feet again, and under the existing conditions that could not be accomplished without allowing capitalist trade relations to operate freely in the countryside. It meant producing goods the peasantry needed and transporting them where they could be traded.

The Bolsheviks made a lot of foolish mistakes, as Lenin said. Especially the city folk who thought that being a socialist meant they knew something about growing food,

"We are pupils of the peasants and not their teachers. Nothing is more stupid than people who know nothing about farming and its specific features, rushing to the village only because they have heard of the advantages of socialized farming, are tired of urban life and desire to work in rural districts—it is most stupid for such people to regard themselves as teachers of the peasants in every respect. . . . The aim is not to expropriate the middle peasant but to bear in mind the specific condition in which the peasant lives, to learn from him methods of transition to a better system, *and not to dare to give orders!*"

The forced collectivization of the Stalin era was the opposite of this strategy of the Bolsheviks under Lenin. Soviet agriculture to this day suffers from the brutal coercive measures that have marked the Stalinist bureaucracy's policies toward the peasantry.

By contrast, the Cuban land reform and economic development plans favoring the rural areas have been carried out in an exemplary manner. The alliance between the workers and peasants has become more solid with every passing year.

Policies implemented during the first year of the Nicaraguan revolution indicate that the FSLN is building on the lessons and modeling itself on the experiences of the Cuban land reform. Planning had begun long before the victory of the insurrection, and the National Institute of Agrarian Reform (INRA) was launched immediately. Twenty-five percent of the arable land, much of the very best, became state property with Somoza's downfall. Most of it is being organized into cooperatives administered by the government and the Association of Rural Workers. Land rents were slashed to a fraction of their former rates and landlords told to rent at those prices or the uncultivated plots would be confiscated and turned over to their former tenants. Debt foreclosures were outlawed and low interest government loans guaranteed.

The ATC, the Association of Rural Workers, has become the strongest of the mass organizations in Nicaragua and played a decisive role in surpassing farm production goals during the first year. Efforts are being made to organize and improve the conditions of workers on the coffee and banana plantations. INRA and the junta have made each move carefully, only after its necessity was established for all to see, including the most recent decision announced July 19 to proceed with the confiscation and distribution of land being kept out of production by the large latifundists. This new stage of the land reform will inevitably bring new confrontations, especially with the cotton plantation owners, one of the most powerful and reactionary sectors of the bourgeoisie.

The National Institute of Agrarian Reform was set up as a way of driving the revolution in the countryside forward despite any opposition. Many of the best cadres of the FSLN were put into INRA precisely because they understood that they had to begin to change the conditions of life for the peasantry rapidly in order to win their support in the inevitable confrontations and hardships that would come as steps are taken to deepen the revolution.

For example, INRA itself began to organize some of the vaccination programs in rural areas without waiting for the Ministry of Health because INRA was in a position to move much more rapidly and effectively.

This is the meaning and importance of the literacy crusade, as well. The poverty and underdevelopment produced by decades of imperialist economic exploitation cannot be overcome in a year or two. While a start can be made, it's more like a promissory note. But there *is* something you can radically alter in very short order. And that is the self-confidence and self-respect of the peasantry and the working class. When the revolutionary government says to them: "You are more important than the big landowners and bosses. You know more about running society in your interests than anyone else. Therefore, you must learn to read and write, the revolution needs you to learn so you can become leaders and administrators and organizers. Only you can change your life, and united we are strong enough to do it."

The self-confidence and pride that develops as masses of the most downtrodden learn to read and write in a few months' time is one of the most powerful weapons of the revolution.

It's useful to think about what a disadvantage the Bolsheviks were at in Russia because the civil war and imperialist invasion prevented them from carrying out their plans for something like the literacy crusades in Cuba, Nicaragua, and Grenada. Illiteracy and the general educational backwardness were a tremendous problem. Lenin stressed that this was the biggest obstacle to drawing the working class into running the economy, administering the state.

The number of "workers who are governing is inordinately, incredibly *small*," he said. "The result of this low cultural level is that the Soviets, which by virtue of their programme are organs of government *by the working people*, are in fact organs of government *for the working people* by the advanced section of the proletariat, but not by the working people as a whole." The educational backwardness helped foster the growth of bureaucracy as well.

Their literacy drives give the Nicaraguan and Grenadian revolutions a qualitative advantage over the Russian—even if, like the Bolsheviks, they suffer from the lack of cadre to fulfill all the tasks. That lack, I suspect, is simply a law of revolution.

The literacy drive in Nicaragua is not only educating hundreds of thousands of people and transforming their self-consciousness and self-respect. It is also developing new cadres of the revolution. The high school and junior high school students who are the backbone of the literacy crusade are getting an education too. Living in the countryside, sharing the conditions the peasants live with year round, deepening their understanding and commitment. In the process, many of the student teachers will learn to be leaders.

All this is in addition to the political content of the educational materials used in the literacy campaign. The Nicaraguan people are learning their own real history as they learn to read and write. They are learning about imperialism and Sandino, about exploitation and the struggle for freedom and human dignity. The textbooks have even been reviewed by the women's association to make sure women are not portrayed as inferior to men, capable of playing only stereotyped "female" roles. The Nicaraguan bourgeoisie has been howling about the content of the textbooks, but their real target is not that. It is not even *what* people are being taught that mainly upsets the bourgeoisie, but the fact that the workers and peasants are being told that they are the most important part of society. That helps alter the very foundation of class relations in Nicaragua. It's another big step by those who were ruled toward becoming the rulers.

The working class

A third basic question on which the vanguard must lead is the homogenization of the political understanding of the working class. The diverse layers of workers go through many experiences as they progressively establish the foundations of a socialist economy and become conscious of themselves as a ruling class. They go through the school of unionization, of workers' control, and learn to think through and answer the political arguments advanced by all the left and right lamebrains within the working class movement.

No unions were allowed to function without harassment and repression under Somoza except company unions and those slavishly dedicated to the defense of the dictatorship and the interests of imperialism. With the overthrow of the regime, trade unions were legalized, and the right to organize was guaranteed in the new Statute of Rights. The Sandinista Workers Federation, the CST, was established alongside other unions already in existence that were led by various Social Democratic, Stalinist and Christian Democratic tendencies. The fight to win the majority of workers to the CST, to support the FSLN, and to support the government, began.

As among the peasantry, this is a political struggle to win the confidence and leadership of the workers. It is a question of convincing, not ordering or abusing the power of the government apparatus. Opponents within the workers' movement, political enemies of the workers' and farmers' government—modern day counterparts of the Mensheviks and Left Socialist Revolutionaries—try to use the real problems facing the government and the workers—economic chaos, deteriorating working conditions, inflation, unemployment—to turn the workers against the FSLN and bring down the revolutionary government.

After the government threw the non-Nicaraguan members of the infamous Simón Bolívar Brigade out of the country last August (but not before this band of sectarian adventurers dragged the name of Trotskyism through the mud), the most serious ultraleft opponents they have had to face have been the CAUS (the Action and Labor Unity Federation), which is led by one of the pro-Moscow organizations, the Communist Party of Nicaragua, and the Frente Obrero, which looks to the Albanian bureaucracy for guidance and inspiration. We know both these types well from our experiences in the labor movement here.

In the early months of the revolution some of the central leaders of these currents were arrested and jailed, because of the inflammatory political content of their propaganda. Later it turned out that the Frente Obrero was also collecting weapons and organizing an armed group. Subsequently, the decision was made by the leadership of the FSLN to release the CAUS and Frente Obrero people from jail and to deal with the problems they create in a different way, as part of the political battle to educate and win the working class.

Like the FSLN, we have no illusions in the character and the role of these groups. They are a menace to the revolution and to the working class. Countering their propaganda and agitation requires a high level of political consciousness on the part of the working class. It is not an easy problem. This, too, is one of the things that Trotsky explained very well in the talk he gave to the Young Communist League in 1922.

Trotsky pointed out: "When a young worker, before the war, under the bourgeois regime went into the workshop, the more advanced workers there would simply explain his position to him thus: 'There's your boss,' they would say, 'he's your enemy, your exploiter. What means do you have to hit back?—The strike.' And the young worker, while still not having the slightest idea what bourgeois society, France, Britain, the Stock Exchange, imperialism, or militarism are, has already received in this small cell his workshop, all the inducement required to form himself into a revolutionary fighter, a conscious proletarian."

But what happens now, Trotsky asked, in the workers' republic?

"Today's young worker in the workshop encounters material conditions which are worse than those that he experienced under capitalism," because of the destruction of the imperialist war and the civil war, and the need to begin the process of primitive accumulation all over.

This means "any Menshevik or SR [Socialist Revolutionary], by repeating what we used to say in front of the bourgeoisie, thrusts the worker on to the path of opposing himself to the working class as a whole. This, comrades, is the kernel of the question. It is a very simple one if you think it over and if you know a little bit about what is the state, what is class and exploitation. But it is just this young worker who has only just come into the factory, who does not know this, while in a bourgeois-capitalist factory whose first movement was correct. Now though he must understand the nature of the Soviet state in order to gain a correct understanding of the conditions of his working life. Now he must become aware of the building of the whole of Soviet society in order to grasp his position in the factory and the workshop."

This is exactly the situation facing the workers of Nicaragua today—and their vanguard. Only the names have changed. Educating and winning the workers away from the influence of those who would destroy the revolutionary government remains the central task.

It is worth noting, too, that those workers supporting the revolutionary government who still work in privately owned enterprises have some of the most difficult tactical problems. How to organize and fight for better wages and working conditions, while not getting crosswise with the broader strategic decisions of national and international politics on when to expropriate remaining capitalist-owned industry. The consciousness of the workers in these enterprises becomes one of the objective factors to be weighed in making those decisions.

It is one of the reasons why in some cases it may be politically correct to nationalize before it would be economically necessary or desirable to do so. This is one of the pressures that will force the leadership to move to resolve the contradictions between the workers' and peasants' government and the remaining capitalist property relations.

Deepening workers' control in the capitalist-owned enterprises becomes an essential school for training the Nicaraguan working class. Organized committees of the workers must be established in all the capitalist enterprises to look into every aspect of the company's operations and determine whether the rule of social needs before profits is being observed by the owners. Only as the workers themselves become increasingly competent to manage the industries that are nationalized can the process go forward from workers' control to workers' management with the least possible dislocation.

In the early months of the Russian revolution the workers in many factories organized to demand their work places be expropriated. "When workers' delegations came to me with complaints against the factory owners," Lenin said, "I always said to them: 'You want your factory nationalized. Well and good. We have the decree ready and can sign it in a moment. But tell me, can you take the organisation into your own hands? Do you know how and what you produce? And do you know the relations between your product and the Russian and international market?' And inevitably it transpired that they knew nothing. There was nothing written about such matters in the Bolshevik textbooks, or even in those of the Mensheviks."

These are the same kinds of problems confronting the workers and peasants and their government in Nicaragua today. How to move forward in resolving some of these difficult questions of class education and class struggle, while making the transition to a nationalized, planned economy in a small, devastated, poor country, in a world still dominated by imperialism.

The biggest mistake we could make in trying to think through the problems facing Nicaragua or Grenada would be to apply prefabricated formulas and tactics derived from other countries at other international conjunctures. We must understand the general laws of economics and their political ramifications. And we must also be able to see what is specific and unique to these countries today. Otherwise we will misjudge the profound revolutionary processes taking place.

In 1921, Lenin greeted the Communist leaders of the Soviet Republics of the Caucasus—Azerbaijan, Georgia, Armenia, Daghestan and the Mountaineer Republic—with some advice that is well worth thinking about. To maintain and develop soviet power, Lenin told them, the most important thing "is that the Communists of the Transcaucasus should be fully alive to the *singularity* of their position . . . that they should appreciate the need to refrain from copying our tactics."

You face different conditions than we had to deal with in Russia, Lenin said. First of all you don't stand alone, Soviet Russia now exists and can help you politically and militarily.

Second, you won't face the same kind of international military intervention because imperialism got its fingers burnt in Russia and will now be more cautious.

Third, the Caucasian Republics have an even more pronounced peasant character than Russia, which means that your tactics must be different.

And fourth, you will be much less isolated economically from the advanced capitalist countries.

"You will need to practice more moderation and caution," Lenin advised, "show more readiness to make concessions to the petty bourgeoisie, the intelligentsia, and particularly the peasantry. You must make the swiftest, most intense and all possible economic use of the capitalist West through a policy of concessions and trade. . . .

"This must be done on a wide scale, with firmness, skill and circumspection, and it must be utilised to the utmost for improving the condition of the workers and peasants, and for enlisting the intelligentsia in the work of economic construction. . . .

"What the Republics of the Caucasus can and must do, as distinct from the R.S.F.S.R., is to effect a slower, more cautious and more systematic transition to socialism. That is what you must understand, and what you must be able to carry out, as distinct from our own tactics.

"We fought to make the first breach in the wall of world capitalism. The breach has been made. . . .

"You, Comrade Communists of the Caucasus, have no need to force a breach. You must take advantage of the favourable international situation in 1921, and learn to build the new with greater caution and more method. In 1921, Europe and the world are not what they were in 1917 and 1918.

"Do not copy our tactics, but analyse the reasons for their peculiar features, the conditions that gave rise to them, and their results; go beyond the letter, and apply the spirit, the essence and the lessons of the 1917–21 experience."

Those words should be emblazoned on the banner of every revolutionary party.

The foreign policy record

With that in mind, let's turn from questions of domestic politics to the world relationship of class forces and take a look at some of the problems of foreign policy that confront a revolutionary government wielding state power in the interests of workers and peasants.

Here I want to focus on Cuba and its foreign policy, because twenty-one years is a more adequate time span to judge by than one year.

The essence of Cuban foreign policy can be summed up very simply. It is proletarian internationalism.

As Fidel summarized it in the report that was adopted by the First Congress of the Communist Party of Cuba in 1975, "The starting point of Cuba's foreign policy . . . is the subordination of Cuban positions to the international needs in the struggle for socialism and for the national liberation of the peoples."

That was the starting point for the foreign policy of the Soviet Union under Lenin and Trotsky; it was reversed under Stalin and his heirs.

This fact, the existence of a revolutionary state power that is carrying out a proletarian internationalist foreign policy is one of the most fundamental features of the world political situation today.

Is this something new?

No, it's not. This has been Cuba's foreign policy from the very first days of the revolution. If you go back over the twenty-year record and review the basic speeches and documents of the revolution, you find this policy repeated and described, illustrated, and implemented over and over again—from the days of the Second Declaration of Havana to this year's July 26 celebration in Cuba.

Is this a fact we have only now discovered?

No. We have always noted that Cuba's stance toward U.S. imperialism has been and remains qualitatively different from all the other workers' states. For twenty-one years Cuba has remained unbought and unbowed.

We did make one mistake during that period. For a number of years, in the early 1970s, we stopped paying close attention to what was going on in Cuba. We stopped reading *Granma* regularly, following the domestic policy discussions, reading their foreign policy speeches carefully. We didn't take advantage of opportunities to visit Cuba, to meet and discuss with Cubans. So we started to drift away from an accurate appreciation of what Cuba was doing and accomplishing on a number of fronts. But we corrected that a couple of years ago, and now we're on the right track.

Is there something new? Yes. The world political situation has changed. U.S. imperialism was defeated in Vietnam. The long postwar boom came to an end bringing a deepening economic crisis for world capitalism. The Portuguese empire in Africa was shattered. The world relationship of class forces shifted to our advantage.

Revolutionary pressures throughout the semicolonial world have mounted.

The capitalist offensive here at home has intensified, while working-class resistance to the economic squeeze and to the drive toward militarization has grown.

The broad shifts in the world situation created the conditions that made possible the victory of the New Jewel Movement in Grenada and the Sandinista triumph in July 1979. They underlie the developing mass insurrectionary struggle in El Salvador today. They have made it possible for the revolutionary leadership in Cuba to move into the breach and help advance the anti-imperialist and anticapitalist struggle on a world scale.

The relative weakening of imperialism added to the mass pressures that are building around the world have made it possible for Cuba to tip the balance in revolutionary struggles in a number of countries. Although a small country with only 10 million people, located in a vulnerable geographic location, Cuba is a giant in world historical terms. It is pursuing a proletarian internationalist foreign policy with the consumate skill of a battle-tested combat leadership. And that, comrades, is why we are heading inexorably toward a deepening confrontation in the Caribbean and Central America. Because the world revolution is on the march. Because imperialism has been weakened, but is still a deadly beast fighting for its life. Because revolutionary internationalism is alive and strong in Cuba, and five million marching people on May 17 proclaimed that their solidarity with Nicaragua, with Grenada, with El Salvador, is not negotiable. It is unconditional. And that is why, as Fidel said recently, Cuba has become a specter that is haunting the Yankees.

Does Cuba want trade relations with the United States? Of course it does. Would it make considerable economic concessions to end the blockade? Of course. But the one condition that the United States demands is the one that Cuba will not meet. The Cubans will not pull back from supporting any people anywhere in the world who are struggling against imperialism, against exploitation, against racism, against oppression. They will not sell their revolutionary honor and integrity for a mess of pottage.

U.S. imperialism's total economic blockade of Cuba for twenty-one years has been a crushing burden. A total blockade, including on all food, medicine, on any product containing nickel mined in Cuba. A prohibition preventing any ship that has stopped in Cuba from docking in an American port. The blockade of Cuba will go down in history as one of the most brutal acts of imperialist aggression ever. Even the blockade of the Soviet Union in the early years only lasted for three or four years.

The Cuban government has correctly tried to exploit every tiny opening, every tiny split or division in the imperialist front. They express genuine appreciation to any government that is willing to stand up to the pressures and sanctions of U.S. imperialism and establish trade relations with Cuba.

Many ultraleft and sectarian opponents of the Cuban leadership have criticized Castro for his public receptions accorded antiworking-class politicians such as the leaders of the Spanish imperialist government and various semicolonial bourgeois regimes. No one has to agree with every word Castro says, and he would be the last to request approval. But if you are going to criticize, you have to start with the right framework. It is not Castro's job to overthrow the Spanish monarch, or organize the masses to dispose of the Mexican bourgeoisie. His job is to maneuver with the imperialist and semicolonial governments to take advantage of their contradictions and conflicts in order to loosen the noose that is around Cuba's neck. His job is to deepen these divisions and secure some trade agreements. If this means smiling and exchanging compliments with thoroughly reprehensible figures, he will only find himself in the company of other dubious proletarian revolutionists like Lenin.

Cuba and the USSR

What about Cuba's relations with the Soviet Union? Here, too, many of the criticisms that are leveled at Cuba flow from a stance toward class politics on a world scale that is so wrong as to give aid and shelter to counterrevolutionaries. Here I am referring to the various state capitalist currents, Maoist groups and other petty-bourgeois sects. We could also toss in the liberal and "Marxist" academics who have been vociferously denouncing the Cuban revolution's supposed degeneration and abandonment of revolutionary internationalism—which they never supported to begin with.

In essence they all charge that because Cuba does not publicly attack the Kremlin as counterrevolutionary, and in fact points to the Soviet workers' state as the "natural ally" of those fighting against imperialism, Cuba is nothing but a puppet of the Kremlin and it, too, must be implementing a counterrevolutionary policy.

In 1970, speaking on the 100th anniversary of Lenin's birth, Castro lashed out at what he called the liberaloids, the charlatans, and superleftists who did not understand the most fundamental fact about the relationships of class forces on a world scale—the objective meaning of the October revolution and the existence of the Soviet workers' state.

"Without the October Revolution of 1917," Castro said, "it would have been impossible for Cuba to become the first socialist country in Latin America!

"We would have been revolutionaries just the same; our country would have gone ahead to the ultimate consequences—there is not the slightest doubt—but the greatest sacrifices, the most heroic decisions would not have prevailed over the consequences of the power of imperialism situated only 90 miles away from our shores; they could not have prevailed over the consequences of imperialism's criminal economic, political and military attacks. . . .

"As we all know, there are today superrevolutionary theoreticians, superleftists, veritable Supermen, if you like . . . capable of disemboweling imperialism in two seconds, in words; many superrevolutionaries who haven't the slightest notion of reality or of the problems and difficulties involved in a revolution; urged on by that feeling nurtured by imperialism, they bear tremendous hatred. It is as if they could not forgive the Soviet Union for existing, and this, from leftist positions. . . .

"The existence of the Soviet state is, objectively—I repeat, objectively—one of the most extraordinary privileges enjoyed by the revolutionary movement."

In what is one of the most interesting passages of this speech, Castro went on:

"What do I mean by this? I mean that it is possible to have different opinions of different problems; I mean that different revolutionary movements may have different interpretations as to how to face certain things. This does not mean that every Party must perforce think exactly the same way as others. No! Let there be no misunderstanding about this. We believe that due to the enormous diversity of problems and the complexity of problems there will always be a great number of different viewpoints. There will always be! To expect anything anything else would be sheer idealism. . . .

"Above everything else, we shall always take into account objective truth and objective values. And we spoke of how decisive Soviet support has been to us.

"And there are some who don't even approve of our mentioning this. What a bunch of disgusting liberaloids there are floating about this world, charlatans who have never had to come face to face with a single problem—to say nothing of the problem of an entire nation—or had to bear the suffering and misery of an entire nation!"

On that basic framework we agree with the Castro leadership. The Cuban workers' state exists today only because the fire of the October revolution is still burning. The survival of Cuba as a force for world revolution depends on its relationship with the Soviet Union. Any other policy would be childish ultraleftism—at best.

Working together within that framework we also agree with Fidel that there are many different viewpoints within the revolutionary movement. We, the Fourth International, come out of a different history than the Castro leadership. And at the appropriate time and place, we would like to discuss some questions we think are important. But that's not where we propose to begin. What is crucial is that we stand shoulder to shoulder in the struggle against our common class enemy, U.S. imperialism, and alongside peoples struggling for their liberation throughout the world. Only in the course of that struggle can the validity of our ideas be tested.

Cuba and the Non-Aligned

What about Cuba's role in the Non-Aligned Movement? That is another facet of their proletarian internationalist foreign policy that draws fire from sectarian critics. But Cuba's starting point is the same as that of the Second Congress of the Communist International, the Leninist line—"Workers of all countries and oppressed nations unite."

Yes, there is a common struggle on the part of all those who suffer the brutality and misery of imperialist domination. They have the same enemy as the workers of the imperialist countries. And the toiling masses of the workers' states are their natural allies. They all have the same interests in combating imperialism.

Does this obliterate class divisions within the oppressed nations? Hardly. No more than the subjugation of all Blacks to racist oppression obliterates the class divisions within the Black population. That's why the banner of the FSLN is inscribed with Sandino's words, "Only the workers and peasants will go all the way." But the fact of imperialist domination means there is an additional dimension to the class struggle in the colonial and semicolonial world. You cannot simply transpose the relations and tactics of the class struggle in the imperialist countries.

The Cubans understand that the struggle against imperialism is one of the most powerful motor forces of the world socialist revolution today. By leading and speaking for that anti-imperialist struggle, by giving the clearest and sharpest expression to the anti-imperialist sentiments of the oppressed masses the world over, the Cubans understand that they can help to mobilize those masses into an even more powerful battering ram against the existing world economic order—i.e., imperialism.

Their line is quite simple. Wherever any man or woman or child is hungry or sick or illiterate, Cuba is there. Wherever any human soul is fighting imperialist domination, Cuba is there. Those are our brothers and sisters, and *because* we were able to break the chains first, we have a debt to humanity, an obligation to help others. That is proletarian internationalism.

One of the most common themes of Fidel's speeches in recent years has been, as he put it on July 26, that "our consciousness" is "foreign to all chauvinism, foreign to all national egoism." If Cubans are fortunate to *have* more, they must *give* more. The workers of the world have no homeland. Cuba speaks—and fights—for every child anywhere in the world who doesn't have even a crust of bread.

It's along that road that Cuba is proving its internationalism. More than *fifty thousand* Cuban doctors, teachers, engineers, and agricultural experts are right now working abroad in more than thirty countries, sharing their knowledge and skills with other victims of imperialist superexploitation and underdevelopment. In doing so, Cuba shows by its example that only the road of socialist revolution can solve the problems of humanity.

The meaning of Mariel

The proletarian internationalism of the Cuban masses is nothing but the extension of economic and social policies within Cuba. And that, more than anything else, is the meaning of the events of the last year inside Cuba. Whatever the bureaucratic deformations that exist in Cuba—and there certainly are some just as there were in the early years of the Soviet Union—what has been demonstrated in the last year is the limits of those deformities. The three mass mobilizations this spring, each over 1 million people, in the space of several weeks. The speeches by Raúl Castro against bureaucratism, loss of nerve, or the search for an easy life. The housecleaning of Mariel. All these indicate the degree to which it is *not* those who have grown weary and tired of the struggle, *not* the "fainthearts" who are setting policy in Cuba. On the contrary, Cuba today is clearly led by those who, together with the central core of the Castro leadership, are saying, "Now we are no longer alone. Everything for Nicaragua. Everything for Grenada. Everything for El Salvador. And those who have grown tired, those who are not with us should leave."

Castro expressed it the most succinctly: "Those who do not have revolutionary genes, who do not have revolutionary blood, who do not have a mind that adapts itself to the idea of a revolution, who do not have a heart that adapts itself to the effort and the heroism of a revolution, we don't need them in our country."

That was the essence of Mariel. It was a real split that extended into former cadres of the revolution. That's why it produced some heat in Cuba—especially against those who were in the CP and had been organizers and had been considered supporters of the revolution, but now wanted to get out of the line of fire. It was a split, a cleansing that leaves the revolution stronger. As Castro put it, "we need not worry if we lose some flab. We are left with the muscle and bone of the people." We're in better fighting trim.

Nothing sums up the domestic and international line of the Cuban revolution more succinctly than Fidel's May Day declaration that building socialism is the task of absolutely free men and women.

What we have to learn

Speaking to Cuban civilian and military volunteers in Luanda, Angola, in 1977, Castro reiterated: "I say this with more conviction than ever—these problems of humanity have no solution without revolution and socialism."

That is the path not only in Latin America, not

only in Central America, not only in Africa and Asia, but in North America too. That is the path that we are on, and we are confident that the American working class will see it through to the end. But we, like the Grenadians, know that we're not making a cup of instant coffee. The tasks that confront us are so enormous that we cannot hope to measure up to them unless we approach every living struggle of our class, especially every victorious socialist revolution, with the spirit of students striving to learn.

We go to the Nicaraguan revolution, to the Cuban revolution, to the Grenadian revolution, to learn—not to teach; to absorb everything we can to better prepare ourselves for the struggles that are coming.

This is not because we think we have nothing to offer. But every revolution is a complex living organism with its own concrete set of class relationships, nationally and internationally. To apply the science of Marxism, we can't just read a book, or study the last revolution, and mechanically transfer its tactics. We have to understand the revolution as an organic, living whole.

Understanding this is closely intertwined with the turn that we are making right here in this country to become a party of industrial workers, to take advantage of the changing political conditions in this country to better prepare ourselves for the class battles that are coming. They will be interconnected with the events that take place in Cuba, Grenada, Nicaragua, El Salvador, Guatemala.

We should have no illusions. Enormous pressures are bearing down on us and on our class as the confrontation in the Caribbean sharpens. They will increase as the American rulers push closer to trying once again to use their military might. They are the same pressures that led 100,000 Cubans to get out of the way, to resign from the struggle for a better world.

The same pressures are coming down on the fainthearts the world over who want to run from the front lines.

The only way that we and other revolutionists can withstand these pressures is by following the course that we have charted here. To be one with our class, to help steel ourselves, in that way, against the vacillators and fainthearts.

We don't minimize the tests that are coming, the scope of the struggle. There are no guarantees. The fate of Nicaragua, Guatemala, Grenada, El Salvador, Cuba—those all will be decided in struggle. As Fidel said, "They can make the struggle costlier, they can make it bloodier and more painful, but there's no way they can prevent it."

What we have been talking about today, the subjective side of this equation, the leadership question, is of crucial importance. When you're going into the trenches, you want to know who's fighting next to you. You want to know who you can count on and who you can't. Your life depends on it.

Unlike the fainthearts, when we hear one and a half million Cubans shouting, "For sure, Fidel, give the Yankees hell!"; when we hear half a million Nicaraguans singing "The children of Sandino do not sell themselves, nor do they surrender"; when we hear our Grenadian brothers and sisters shout "Forward ever, backward never, four hundred years is enough!"—our spirits soar. Because we know that we're going into battle with the most powerful allies on the face of this earth. With millions of men and women and young people who are fighting for the very future of humanity.

Our fellow revolutionists around the world, throughout the Caribbean and Central America are looking at us too, trying to size us up in the same way. To them we say that we will do everything in our power to help defend and extend their revolutions, which are part of our revolution. But we too are revolutionists of action. We try to learn the lessons of history as best we can. But it's what we do in the test of big events that matters.

And that is how we hope to be judged.

MARXISM AND THE CLASS STRUGGLE TODAY

By Jack Barnes

Everyone who has heard the reports on the world political situation and on the revolutions in Central America and the Caribbean, and who participated in the rally last night in solidarity with those revolutions, has to be convinced not only that the international relationship of class forces has shifted in our favor, but also that there are growing opportunities to take further steps in humanity's long march toward a human and socialist world.

In the capitalist world today, increasing instability lies underneath whatever surface calm exists. Unexpected explosions erupt. The ruling capitalist class, spurred by competition and weakened by lagging economies, is everywhere on an offensive against the conditions under which working people must live and work. Everywhere the rulers are probing the weaknesses of the toilers' organizations. The imperialists threaten the use of force and build up more massive arsenals. The continual operation of the secret political police reveals the class nature of capitalist democracy and its growing strains as class polarization deepens.

But something else became clearer in the last couple of days, something that is going on beneath the surface. In the face of setbacks, the workers are becoming more politicized, more resistant to the capitalist attacks, more open to the idea that the current methods of the leaderships of their mass organizations are not effective. They are becoming more skeptical of "official"—that is, bourgeois—politics, while at the same time more interested in broad political questions.

On a world scale, it is becoming more and more evident to the masses of toilers that, as the Sandinistas say, "Only the workers and farmers will go all the way." Confidence in the political parties of the bourgeoisie begins to decline. The farmers, the urban poor, the women, the oppressed nationalities, the revolutionary-minded students hunt for ways to link up with the power of the working class. The desire and ability to act and to change things, to take advantage of the changed relationship of forces, increases.

Our tasks as internationalists are obvious: to organize international solidarity with these struggles, to draw inspiration from them, to become knowledgeable about and learn from them, to deepen our personal and collective commitment to act in their defense.

But as important and necessary as these tasks are, they are secondary to understanding and acting on another fact: this change in the *world* class relationship of forces is also a change *right here* in the United States, in the mines and the mills and the plants, and in all politics. The United States is not merely situated in an increasingly revolutionary world, but itself basically *different* from that surrounding world. Our tasks are not limited to learning how to relate to an increasingly explosive, class-polarized world, *out there*. We're an *integral part* of that world. What we are seeing, what we're living through and have the opportunity to participate in, is not just the crisis and breakup of the imperialist system of domination that came in with the twentieth century, but a crisis of capitalism and capitalist rule. In the 1980s revolutionary perspectives are the only realistic perspectives—throughout the world, and right here at home. And unlike the 1930s, when revolutionary perspectives were also realistic in the United States, there is a different—a more favorable—relationship of class forces on a world scale.

This talk was given at the Socialist Educational and Activists Conference in Oberlin, Ohio, August 4, 1980.

The world features that we've discussed—growing instability, unexpected explosions, attacks on the working class, the threat of the use of force abroad, and the operations of the political police, the politicization of the workers going on beneath the surface, the growing class polarization, and the declining confidence in the bourgeoisie and its parties—all these are occurring, and will occur more in the United States itself.

The ruling class has fewer and fewer options. Its hand is forced by the unfolding laws of motion of capital. (That sounds like one of those "hackneyed Marxist phrases," as they say in editorials in the daily press, but that's exactly what forces their hand.) The *focus* of the ruling class attacks is shifting. Five years ago the attacks focused on the weakest of the oppressed and exploited. They began by chipping away at social gains and benefits. They zeroed in on the weakest unions. But more and more, the focus of the attacks shifts towards their strategic target, the industrial working class and its organizations. The closings and threats of closing major plants, bankruptcy threats, and the blackmail of the workers flowing from these are at the center of the attacks. These weapons flow from the historic needs of American capital to restructure its industry to compete with its international rivals. Buffers to the economic effect of these attacks—beginning with social welfare, and going through things like SUB funds and special T.R.A. [Trade Relief Act] unemployment benefits—will sooner or later be cut back even more.

This is a combined offensive, against the American workers and against the workers on a world scale. The ruling class is waging a battle for registration and the draft. It is also a battle for the "right" to be able to fight a Vietnam War in Central America and the Caribbean—or in the Mideast, Africa, or South Asia. It's one and the same fight by the ruling class. And the same is true from the point of view of our class.

This is transforming the working class. The 1970s have not been as sensational from the point of view of most bourgeois and petty bourgeois writers and commentators as were the 1960s. To these people the 70s were more boring. They were the age of narcissism, the search for self, etc. But this is only the appearance. The most important thing about the 70s in this country is not so much what *happened* but what was *prepared* in the minds of the American proletariat. American workers became more open to the real facts of class society and to new answers about them. They felt class differences sharpen. That's the reality.

Jerry Rubin finds a home

In the 1970s we entered a period in which, without a clear working-class perspective, you couldn't have the faintest idea of what was happening. I read an article just prior to this conference written by an old acquaintance of ours—Jerry Rubin. It announced that Jerry Rubin had just accepted a job with a Wall Street firm as a securities analyst. He says, "I know I can be more effective today wearing a suit and a tie and working on Wall Street than I can be dancing outside the walls of power. . . . As the 80s dawned, I found myself becoming bored with the mobility and personal freedom that I had cherished for the last 20 years. I felt separated from power."

He explains, "In the United States, the radical dream of transforming the system from the outside had floundered, then virtually disappeared. . . . My friends from that period have gone in thousands of apparently unconnected directions." Rubin goes on, "Politics and rebellion distinguished the 60s. The search for the self characterized the spirit of the 70s. Money and financial interest will capture the passion of the 80s."

He ends up, "Let's make capitalism work for everyone."

I think he's come to believe this. And much of what he says is true from the point of view of the petty bourgeoisie slavishly dependent upon capital—the power that he sees dominating this country. But it's not true that the directions his friends went off in were unconnected. The directions they all went off in were connected by their total lack of connection with the working class and its revolutionary perspectives. To him and his friends—hundreds of thousands of them—the seventies did become the search for the inner self. And their age of narcissism stretches into the eighties. They did find themselves more and more bored with their "personal freedom" and "mobility." And nothing could capture better the chasm between what happens to different classes at turning points in history.

The working class did not enter the search for the inner self. The working class was pounded into searching for solidarity *among ourselves* in the seventies, to prepare for the eighties. The working class didn't become bored with the mobility and personal freedom we had in the seventies. We were taught in the seventies that the little mobility and personal freedom we had was disappearing with the economic crisis, and we would have to fight to maintain it. The working class didn't *lose* any "radical dream" of transforming American society. Many workers became open for the first time to *thinking about* the possibility of radically transforming American society. The workers did not become convinced in the seventies that "capitalism can work for everyone." To the contrary, it is this very proposition that workers have become more dubious about. Today, only a class-conscious viewpoint from within the struggles of the working class itself can allow you to even *see* the reality—what is and what is coming. Mistake after mistake, blunder after blunder, and reactionary position after reactionary position, will follow for anyone who doesn't.

As the 1980s open, the appearance and the reality are not the same. We must understand this.

Washington gets a message

Since we are gathered in a chapel, to illustrate this point I will take as my text this morning the banner headline from this week's *Militant*. It says, "Carter Registration Drive a Huge Fiasco." Another version of this headline could be "Bourgeoisie Gets a Message From Our Class." It was "Hell no, we won't die for Texaco." In the two weeks when young America was supposed to register for the draft, Carter and those he serves bumped into the reality of what the seventies produced. They bumped into the reality of the American working class today.

It reminded me of what happened to the mine owners a couple of years ago, when they tried to kick the miners out of shape as the first step in the rulers' direct assault on the industrial working class. They bumped up against the power of the miners underneath the UMWA officialdom, and they found that it wasn't so simple. It's similar to the message Tenneco got from the Newport News steelworkers.

That's what just happened with the initial two weeks of the registration drive. This was revealed not only by the numbers who refused to register—those who said, "we'll just let it slide for now"—but also by those who registered while making it clear they have no intention of fighting and dying for Texaco. And even many of those who joined the army—during what the army called the recent months of "dynamite recruiting"—explained they were joining what they considered a peacetime army because they couldn't find jobs, and they have no intention of doing any fighting.

This is the opposite of the situation at the beginning of the Vietnam War. Today, far from seeing those who say no to even registering as shirkers or cowards or weirdos, millions of young workers respect them. And these registration refusers are, in their majority, young workers. They know they did the dying in the last one—and if they're Black or Latino they know they did even more than their share of the dying.

This two weeks of registration was the culmination of a political defeat for the American ruling class. It wasn't a military defeat, of course; there is nothing military going on yet. It wasn't a definitive defeat; the campaign to politically convince young America to get ready to die for the employers will be renewed. But it was a real political defeat. We are in the middle of an awesome historical contradiction. On the one side there is the unprecedented military power of American imperialism; on the other, their political difficulties in being able to use that power to crush the world revolution.

If you look only at the surface, like Jerry Rubin, you would have a different idea of what's going on. I don't know how many of you remember Carter's "State of the Union" speech, in January of this year, when he announced the registration drive. It was a genuine war speech. It was the first real war speech of the Carter administration—rough, tough, peanut plantation talk. And if you based your view of reality on his words, which do reflect the intentions and goals of the ruling class, you would think we were on the verge of war. But the entire registration campaign went basically downhill from that night on.

What was involved was not a war speech to initiate *registration*. What was involved was a move by the ruling class to start to wage a fight with you and millions like you, to convince you to accept and support the *draft*, as necessary to build a massive imperialist army for *use in war.* That's what the political fight is about. The administration can never win such a fight just on registration. If there is not going to be a draft, if you don't need a draft, if you don't want a draft, then why register? If they tell you to register, you know damned well they are going to try and draft you. And they are going to have a draft only if they intend to fight a war.

The only way this registration campaign could have been successful would have been to politically win the American people to support the draft. After Carter's initial speech, in face of the negative response to the idea of a draft, the administration backed away from conducting such a fight. Capitalist politicians and the press became divided. The *New York Times* went from initial support for registration to opposition.

I knew something had changed when I heard over the radio in upstate New York the ads that told you to go register. Early in the morning I turned on the radio and Lou Rawls says "Hey man, I'm against the draft too." That's the opening sentence in the ad. I thought some antidraft group had taken out time on the radio station. He repeated this idea a couple of times and then he finally got to the point, "but we have to register," because you never know when someone may start a war against the country.

In New York City there was another ad on Spanish-language television. A young fellow, 19 or 20 years old, runs out his door, throws his suitcase in the trunk of his car, slams the trunk down, and starts to get in the car. His father comes running out, "Son, son, where are you going?" The son replies, "I'm heading for Canada." "No, no, son, it's not a draft, it's just registration."

That wasn't very convincing either.

We saw something we haven't seen since the high point of the struggle against the Vietnam War.

The federal court decision declaring the registration law unconstitutional was not simply accidental. It reflected the sharp tactical division in the ruling class—not on their desire for a draft, not on their desire to draft women if they can get away with it—but on how far along they are in politically winning over the working class to a war perspective. Even the *New York Times* reflected the pressures and divisions, like it used to in the old Vietnam War days. An early Sunday edition—the day before registration was to begin—said, on the front page, that those who do not register will be doing nothing illegal:

"Even if a Justice of the Supreme Court should grant a stay requested later in the day by the Justice Department, the three-judge panel's nullification of the draft statute means that registration will be without force of law, because the special court's ruling that the law was unconstitutional cannot be stayed," the *Times* said.

You can just hear the high level phone calls from Washington to New York when the White House read that! So the next edition said, "An article in today's *New York Times*, based on erroneous information from a lawyer for the plaintiffs, stated incorrectly that registration would be without the force of law in the event of a stay by a Supreme Court Justice."

But even in this revised edition the reporter got in this sentence: "Some constitutional lawyers said, however, that those who did not register would be in a 'very defensible' position."

What occurred was a genuine spontaneous mass action of a certain kind. Without a single mass organization promoting it, without the endorsement of any large organization, the American working people said, "no thank you," at thousands of post offices across the country from the big cities to mining towns and to farm communities.

There was a joke in one of the papers that if this is Carter's answer to the invasion of Afghanistan, the Russians must really be smiling. But the truth of the matter is the Russians aren't smiling that much. Brezhnev is not that happy with this kind of thing. His starting point is not opposition to the imperialist draft. His starting point is good relations with Washington, with the Soviet and U.S. armies in a stand-off. In fact, the Soviet bureaucracy centered its propaganda on the attempted Olympic boycott, not on Carter's decision to try to use the pretext of Afghanistan to get the draft started again. But I can guarantee you that there are workers and peasants in El Salvador and in Vietnam who are grinning about the political failure of registration. And if Brezhnev is not grinning, Fidel is.

What we learned

We have some important lessons to absorb from what happened.

This is especially true because we didn't anticipate accurately the scope of the rejection of the draft on this round. This was exemplified in an article called "What Strategy to Fight the Draft?" in the July 18 *Militant*, which appeared just before the week when registration opened. It was written as the result of a discussion and decision made in the Political Committee.

The article outlined the real purpose of the administration's registration law and propaganda campaign and why our basic slogans center around the theme of "No Draft, No Way, No U.S. Intervention," "Hell no, we won't go, we won't die for Texaco," "Abolish Registration." That was all correct. The fact that registration was the opening battle in a political fight over the draft and not the final decisive battle, was explained accurately.

But we were wrong on a number of things. We said, "Demanding that youth not register will inevitably cut these demonstrations off from many who sign up." That turned out to be false. The many who signed up, who were in their overwhelming majority against the draft and against more Vietnams, were not cut off from those who refused to register. They had many of the same basic views as those who tilted the other way, and who didn't register this time.

We said, "In a confrontation between the Carter administration and those presently willing to refuse to register, the outcome would be gloomy indeed." The outcome was not gloomy whatsoever. It was of historic importance.

We said, "Civil disobedience actions at post offices to stop registration have a logic that tends to turn registrants and antidraft protesters against each other." But almost none of the actions were civil disobedience actions pitting demonstrators against registrants. Most of them took the form of people talking to and arguing with each other about the meaning of the registration and the draft, and they tied together the young generation more than they tore it apart. There were many reports of registrants joining the protests or expressing their antidraft feelings in other ways.

We criticized the *Guardian* for saying "the cutting edge of the political struggle during the two-week registration period in July will be the confrontation between draft registration refusers and the Carter administration." Well, they were at least half correct, if not totally correct. The confrontation was between *all* of those who were against the draft and against any war, and the Carter administration. But a significant component of the advance guard were those who said "No, I'm not registering this time, let it slide." It's not only the Cubans who can judge the shifts in the relationship of class forces and divisions among the oppressors and act flexibly. It's also quite a few nineteen and twenty year olds.

We also said that urging youths not to register would place "the entire burden of stopping Washington's war" on the shoulders of the nineteen and twenty year olds. Well, of course, pushed to its ridiculous extreme, that could be true. But it is not what happened. Those who didn't register felt support from their friends, their families, their co-workers. Their action will affect others, impelling them to think more deeply about it, and to absorb—no matter how little they analyze it—the political fiasco of the registration.

No one feels a great, patriotic, two-week binge of draft registration has just occurred in this country. In fact you can't even find out much about what happened by reading the papers. And the government says they won't even have the figures until November. In other words, the ruling class wants to wait until the elections are over to begin to debate how to relaunch their campaign for political support for draft registration.

We said, "The situation would be different, of course, if a broad antidraft, antiwar movement already existed, with unions and civil rights groups *organizing* their members to massively refuse to register. . . ." Of course, that *would* be different. And that can develop. But without any mass organization at all, a vanguard of American working-class youth knew how to say, "no thank you, not this time."

What conclusions can we draw from this experience?

One conclusion is, don't fight the last war. Don't assume that things will be like they were before. During the Vietnam War there was an existing draft inherited from the period of the Cold War.

Draft resisters were a very narrow category to begin with. That's *not* the situation we now face.

The key question we should have asked ourselves was not, "Is there a great upsurge of people talking about not registering?" But rather, "Is there any indication that workers we know, those we live and work among, are going to flock to register in preparation for conscription, at this stage, under this little pressure, after this amount of debate?"

An important lesson is that we don't assume any defeats at any stage in this struggle against imperialist militarism. We do not know how long it will take them to reinstitute the draft. We don't even know how long it will take them to get the registration going. And every fight is important. Every fight is a fight for the Grenadians, for the Nicaraguans, for the Salvadorean revolution, for the Iranian revolution.

Of course, if the unions and the big civil rights groups organized and led this resistance to the draft, it would be great. Many other things would then also change. This organized form of the resistance doesn't exist yet, because of the character of the current union leadership. But the moods, and attitudes of the working class in the 1980s are going to find ways of overflowing the mass organizations and registering themselves in spite of the misleadership, and this in turn will deeply affect the unions and other mass organizations. We can't predict how this will happen, but it will happen.

We have to be very careful not to confuse our correct rejection of individual draft resistance as a strategy with the concrete tactical decision that has to be made according to the situation at the time.

A rather important conclusion is that we should not be in a rush to reach concrete tactical decisions before we have to. The more we can see and feel of the unfolding situation, the more accurate we will be. What is going to happen certainly cannot be deduced from the positions of the officials of mass organizations.

If we had waited for the weekend before registration opened to make our final decision on tactics—including whether revolutionary socialists should register under protest or refuse to register that coming week—we would have made the correct decision. The manifest split in the ruling class, the court decision declaring the registration law unconstitutional, and other evidence was overwhelming by then. And we would have had this week's interview with comrade John Wood, "Why I'm Not Registering for the Draft," two weeks ago.

Above everything, we have to absorb who was decisive in this confrontation. It was not the students, it was not the pacifists, although many students joined the protests and are opposed to the draft, and many pacifists played a progressive role in refusing to register and counseling others as to their rights. What was decisive was the weight of the young workers of the United States. That's who turned that two weeks into a political defeat for the ruling class. They were decisive—those who declined to register, as well as those who did but are determined not to take part in another Vietnam.

This fact reaffirms and reinforces the correctness of the decision of the YSA and of the party to become a movement composed overwhelmingly of industrial workers. That's the only way we can get a more accurate feel for the real relationship of class forces in the years that are ahead of us, and the only way we can be an effective part of the major political battles.

Moods of the working class are not always on the surface and are often not broadcast publically ahead of time. It's easier to go to a student union to interview youth than to try to accurately probe the views of a cross section of young workers. But that's what we must do and what we must put a priority on doing.

And another message

The registration fiasco wasn't the only message young workers sent recently to the ruling class. Another message was sent from Miami, Chattanooga, Orlando, and other cities. These explosions took on much the same form as those in the 1960s. But they had a different meaning. More and more workers see these explosions not only as Black rebellions but as working people's rebellions. The composition of the participants was not that different, but the effect of the 1970s can be seen here too.

In the same article I referred to earlier, Jerry Rubin also solidarized himself with Andrew Young's confident prediction that Black people are going to "integrate the money" in the 1980s. Maybe, for Rubin and Young, maybe if they crawl enough.

No, that's not what the ruling class has in store for Black people or for most of us, or what the last half decade began teaching us. Unemployed youth would be very happy to give up their "mobility" for a job. And far from "integrating the money," they'll be seeking effective ways to fight racism and economic catastrophe—and they'll do it by any means necessary. Chattanooga is not the last city that will see the cops driven out of working-class areas.

Jesse Jackson, at the PUSH convention, said we know they have two alternatives for Blacks when we're unemployed: send us off to war or lock us up in jail when we protest. That's not only true for Blacks. As the economic crisis deepens, that becomes true for workers in general.

What is beneath these explosions is not only racist brutality and injustice but unemployment, inflation, rotten housing, worthless education—capitalism's evils that face the *entire* working class. What was different in 1980 from the 1960s, among other things, was the attitude of the white workers. These rebellions not only increased respect for Blacks, and even evoked some sympathy—that happened earlier in the 1960s. But there was a partial identification by some non-Black workers with the grievances of Blacks, viewing many of them as just, and even seeing some of them as their own grievances. To the degree the rebellions spoke for all workers and warned all exploiters. These rebellions were previews of coming attractions initiated by a young vanguard of the American working class.

Impact of world revolution

The PUSH convention registered in part the impact of the world events we have been discussing. As the *Militant* reported: "Dessima Williams, Grenada's ambassador designate to the Organization of American States, speaking to the international women's luncheon said, 'Our history is not too different from that of people of color in the United States.'

"Williams hailed Caribbean revolutionary heroes from Haiti's Toussaint L'Overture to Cuba's Che Guevara and explained the need to extend the revolution throughout the Caribbean and around the world.

"Warning of the U.S. government's preparations for war in Central America and the Caribbean, she called for solidarity with the workers and peasants of El Salvador." [*Militant*, August 8, 1980, p. 15.]

That's the kind of leaders we need. Their example is what we have to emulate. The convention also stressed the fight for women's rights and the methods of not registering, the methods of going into the street, the methods of rebelling—these are the only methods that young workers under these conditions have right now. And these methods have their good effects.

They are methods every farm boy and girl knows. When you haven't had time to train him yet, and he won't listen, you can always hit a mule over the head with a two-by-four and get his attention. The events of the last month have resulted in some attention being gotten, not only in the ruling class, but among the misleaders of the working-class movement.

No mass organizations, under their current leaders, speak for the young workers in this country. The Democrats and Republicans do not speak for them. There's a wonderful quote in the *Militant*—a Chattanooga citizen saying, "The only time we ever got anything is right behind a riot."

No, those who rebelled in Miami and elsewhere were not hoodlums. And the daily papers that called them hoodlums didn't really believe it, they wouldn't be so worried if they did. They were young workers, and they were backed by a lot of older workers, like the good, elderly Christian lady packing a .38 on a Miami bus because she'd had enough. That's what they were.

Let's look at the impact of the revolutions in Nicaragua and Grenada from another point of view. Their impact will be different from the first stages of the Cuban revolution, because there are *different conditions* in the world, including the United States. The Cuban revolution conquered at a time when the United States was beginning ten years of uninterrupted economic expansion. There were jobs, and there was an expansion of spending on social programs. There was even the so-called Alliance for Progress, a promise of large-scale economic aid for development in Latin America, launched by the Kennedy Administration in response to the Cuban revolution. Thinly concealed beneath the Alliance for Progress was Washington's political ability to use massive military might to try to crush the Cuban revolution and prevent its extension. They did not succeed in crushing Cuba; but they invaded Santo Domingo, assassinated Che, and did block the extension of the revolution for 20 years.

But the situation is different today. The prolonged economic boom is over. Where there were expanding job opportunities, now there is expanding long-term unemployment. Where there was a growth in social services, now there are cruel cutbacks. There can be no new Alliance for Progress, even as a propaganda maneuver—the economic obstacles are too great. And the U.S. ruling class has yet to win the political fight at home to be able to directly use massive military violence.

We can take the lessons of these revolutions to our class in a way that was not possible a generation ago, when the Cubans triumphed. Compared to the United States, Cuba, Nicaragua and Grenada are economically backward. But they are wonderful examples for us, nevertheless. Lenin kept saying, tell the workers in the West they should do it like we did in Russia, only they'll do it a lot better. A lot better. We're very poor, we make a lot of mistakes. They will do it even better than us.

It's not ultraleft to say there are hundreds of thousands of young workers here in the United States who at least would listen to the idea that what they have done in Cuba and what they are doing in Nicaragua and Grenada about unemployment, inflation, education, health care, housing, the attitude towards other people around the world, racism, women's oppression—should be done here. And we *can* do it better here.

In discussing one of the aspects of how we could do it better here, Trotsky pointed out that there "is no reason why these groups [the lower middle classes in the U.S.] should counterpose determined resistance to the revolution; they have nothing to lose, providing, of course, that the revolutionary leaders adopt a farsighted and moderate policy toward them. . . .

"The same method would be used to draw small businesses and industries into the national organization of industry. By soviet control of raw materials, credits and quotas of orders, these secondary industries could be kept solvent until they were gradually and without compulsion sucked into the socialized business system.

"Without compulsion! The American soviets would not need to resort to the drastic measures that circumstances have often imposed upon the Russians. In the United States, through the science of publicity and advertising, you have means for winning the support of your middle class that were beyond the reach of the soviets of backward Russia with its vast majority of pauperized and illiterate peasants." (*Writings of Leon Trotsky, 1934–35,* Pathfinder Press, 1971, 1974, p.130, p.131, [2011 printing]).

These revolutionaries of action in the Caribbean who are leading the working masses to solve problems that seem more and more insoluble here, are going to have a deeper and deeper effect on working people in this country. We here who are taking the initiative to talk about their actions on the job, at public meetings, in our press, through our election campaigns, are going to find a growing response. Radical-minded workers are going to start seeing that Fidel Castro speaks for the great majority of humanity—including the workers and farmers of the United States—and that he is the kind of leader with guts and brains we need.

They are going to conclude the working class needs its own foreign policy—toward the Caribbean and Central America, toward the whole world—like it needs its own party. And many will start to see that socialism can only be built by free men and women, and that socialism is exactly what free men and women need to build in a world like this.

Right now, the American workers are objectively acting as the allies of these revolutions, the allies of Marxist-led revolutions! That's what they're doing, in fact, by saying no to Vietnam-type wars, no to the draft, no to being crushed without a fight by the capitalist offensive. They are tying the hands of the mortal enemy of the entire planet.

Impact on unions

We have to look at the unions in a new light today, too. The effects on the union movement of the world crisis of capitalism are different than before. The workers need the unions *more*, even with the weaknesses they have stemming from the misleadership of the bureaucracy. As the brutal—and it's brutal—capitalist assault centers more and more on the industrial unions, this lesson will be increasingly driven home.

The effects of the new situation on the unions are expressed in sharply contradictory ways. A few years ago we described the unions as the most conservative organizations in the United States, and, with the obvious qualifications we made at the time, this statement was correct. But now we see that the unions, to give one example, have become the main organizations, outside of women's organizations, that are identified with the ERA. One of the biggest unions, the Steelworkers, took up the fight for affirmative action around the *Weber* case, something unthinkable a few short years before. More are identifying with the antinuclear fight. Now, for their own reasons, the Steelworkers officers have put the question of nationalization of the steel industry on the agenda of their convention.

Comrades from Pittsburgh showed me editorials from the capitalist papers about this. Of course, the editors explain that this proposal is not really meant to be serious, that it is a ploy to campaign with the steel barons to convince the Administration to give help to the steel industry. But the editorials point out, even raising such questions is dangerous. When you put up for debate questions like nationalization, the effect can be quite different from what you intended. That's a problem, but it's their problem and not our problem.

At the same time that you see these changes you see the continuing disastrous results of the current misleadership of the unions. Sam Church's announcement that maybe this year, for the first time in the history of the miners, it won't be "No contract, no work" is just one example. The brutal unfeeling dissolution of District 26 of the United Steelworkers, centered in Youngstown, is another. The USWA tops just accepted the closing of the mills there. They became another group to callously turn their backs on the steelworkers of the Mahoning Valley.

The bureaucracy gives no answers to the catastrophe facing the workers. But it is important to see that struggles and forces that appear to be totally outside the unions—the battle against registration and the draft; Miami and Chattanooga; the battle against nukes; the impact of revolutionary developments in the class struggle in Central America and the Caribbean—are also inside the labor movement itself. The forces involved in these issues are also in the plants and in the unions. These are labor issues.

We should not forget that a revolutionary perspective involves a grasp of the explosive character of the class struggle. People like Michael Harrington and other "socialists" in the labor movement, give the impression that somehow we'll get socialism through rational argument and the approval of Douglas Fraser. We, of course, are all for rationality and argument, and we argue rationally. But that's not the main point.

Lenin had a wonderful attack on those people. He said that "To imagine that the social revolution is *conceivable* without revolts by small nations . . . without revolutionary outbursts by a section of the petty bourgeoisie *with all its prejudices*, without a movement of the [as yet] non-conscious proletarian and semi-proletarian masses against oppression by the landowners, the church, the monarchy, against national oppression, etc.—to imagine all this is to *repudiate social revolution*." With a few additions and changes, that applies in this country too. "Whoever expects a 'pure' social revolution will *never* live to see it," he added. "The socialist revolution . . . *cannot be* anything other than an outburst of mass struggles on the part of all and sundry oppressed and discontented elements." [*Collected Works*, Vol. 22, pp. 355–56.]

The unorganized resistance and opposition to the draft, the Miamis, are signs of young workers breaking through the limits on struggles imposed by the stranglehold on the unions by the "responsible" leaders, although this is not yet manifested in organized form in the unions themselves.

The advantage of boldness

We can add another lesson. And that's what we learned in the petitioning campaign we conducted in many states to get Andrew Pulley, Matilde Zimmermann and other SWP candidates on the ballot. That convinced us personally and directly about the changes taking place in the working class. We simply walked up to fellow workers and talked to them about what's happening in the country and why they should help socialists get on the ballot, and we got a new response. One lesson that we draw from this is to be *bold*. To be bold in what we do, in how we talk, and what we talk about. This experience again affirmed that it is very important not to assume that the surface is the reality.

To a large degree, we get out of talking to fellow workers what we put into it. Don't assume that silence is disagreement. Don't assume that someone's first remark means a thought-out position. Assume that if our analysis is correct, there are hundreds of thousands, if not millions of workers silently considering the big political, economic and social questions, in a deeper way than even two or three years ago.

The change in the world relationship of forces is reflected in this change in the American working class. This change that allows new socialist revolutions to conquer is reflected here in changes in the thinking of American workers—more slowly and in a disguised form, but there nonetheless. The response to Pulley/Zimmermann t-shirts and buttons will by themselves get some good discussions going.

At the same time, the capitalists are inflicting real defeats on the workers. Without any sort of class-struggle union or political leadership, defeats, setbacks of different kinds, blows continue to rain down on the workers. The capitalists are turning the screws. But as they do, class tensions rise, the radicalization and politicization of the more combative workers increases.

We've printed some good reports in the last couple of years on the work of our fractions. One was the report given by Ken Shilman and adopted by the national miners fraction, which was published a couple of months ago. [See *Party Organizer*, Vol. 4 No. 1.]

The report discusses how by working collectively in fractions we can become bold worker-Bolsheviks, establish ourselves as socialists on the job, operate effectively and intelligently, and build a Marxist current.

It explains the importance of keeping our eyes on the young workers in industry. It explains how we can draw out the need for solidarity, for democracy in the unions, and for a political instrument—a labor party.

Ken was disappointed about the reaction of a number of comrades to the section of the report containing the analysis and correction of an error we made in a mine in Birmingham. It was an important error to correct because it was a costly one. But there has been overgeneralization about that error sometimes, abstracting the lesson from the concrete peculiarities the comrades found themselves in. There was no general overall leftist error in our work in the mines—or in any other industry—which this report was designed to correct. In fact, to the contrary, the report explains how American Marxist miners are operating as revolutionary socialists in a growing number of mines around the country.

Engels said one of his great disappointments in so many of the German Marxist comrades was they lacked political cunning. Jim Cannon said it a different way—that any correct policy can be carried out foolishly. But if your byword is boldness, and you believe that what is politically happening in your class is part of what is happening in the world, and you collectively and intelligently organize to carry out the activities appropriate to that political reality, there will be great rewards. We are taking our baby steps, but we are moving forward.

Even during the recession, we are getting new comrades in the mines. We are getting more comrades in rail and aerospace. And when the economy turns up, as it will, the capitalists will hire a lot more. And we'll be among them.

Predict no forms

We often talk about the class-struggle left wing that we want to build, but an important thing to remember about it is we have no concrete form in mind. The class struggle left wing is not yet an organization. Today, the relationship of forces between our class and the enemy class is manifested concretely in the relationship between the fighting workers and the class-collaborationist misleaders within the union movement. That relationship is improving, and from that point of view, progress is being made toward a class-struggle left wing. It will find its organized form when the time comes. Our fight to carry out the policies that lead to building a Marxist tendency is the most important thing we can do now along this road. When, as today, there is a total lack of mass organized forms through which the vanguard workers can move, struggles often take the shape of spontaneous and seemingly chaotic explosions. But these are not just explosions and not just chaos. They are expressions of the growing class polarization, and necessary steps towards the creation of more organized forms (although, as we already discussed, Lenin pointed out that such explosive manifestations will continue at all stages as wider layers enter the struggle).

Retooling and relearning

The increasing class polarization deepens the importance of making our vanguard party a party of workers, of industrial workers increasingly at the center of politics. This is bringing us all kinds of new opportunities. It brings all sorts of pressure too. We are living through the first recession since our turn. We have gone through some rough experiences, and we are still going through some rough spots. No one is so foolish not to see that, know that, and appreciate that. But we are learning completely new lessons. We are retooling. We are retraining. We are relearning again from a new perspective what we formerly learned.

Living through this period of big developments in the class struggle here and abroad, through the shocks, dislocations, and blows felt by the working class, as worker-Bolsheviks within and part of the industrial proletariat, has been like being picked up by the scruff of the neck and shaken by these powerful forces. That's what happens to working-class revolutionaries in a period like this.

Of course, some people after being shaken by the scruff of the neck, take off. They didn't realize what they were getting into. Others, those we're interested in, say, "Thanks, I needed that. I see reality better now." But even these revolutionaries have to fight their way through the confusion of the surface chaos of accelerating events.

For this reason, we need to both deepen the political and theoretical conquests we made in the 60s and 70s and to continue our industrial turn, deepening our proletarian composition and political perspective. In addition we need an organized, systematic effort to educate and reeducate ourselves as Marxists. This must be given the same importance.

The programmatic continuity of our movement is the working class's single most irreplaceable asset, tool, and weapon. The key to our understanding Marxism today is to understand that we have to relearn it. We have to study it from the vantage point of a party more and more part of the proletariat, in the new situation in the world and in this country in which the proletariat is more and more at the center of politics. We have to learn and relearn Marxism as participants in this class struggle.

Marxism looks at itself in class terms. Marxism is the inheritance that the politically conscious members of our class receive from the cumulative lessons of the history of our class in struggle.

Marxism was born along with our class. A new class of working people, the industrial proletariat, what Engels called the hereditary proletariat, was brought into being by capitalism and began fighting for its interests. A lot of revolutionary-minded men and women responded to the potential inherent in the struggle of this new class, but none in the way Marx and Engels did.

The class struggle itself is not new. It has gone on for thousands of years, and many thinkers saw that classes existed and were locked in struggle. What Marx and Engels saw that was new was that the struggle between capital and the new class of industrial proletarians will inevitably culminate in the dictatorship of the proletariat. It will do so, not because anyone wills it or wants it, but because capitalism creates all of the necessary conditions for its own overthrow, including the instruments of this overthrow, its gravediggers, the industrial proletariat.

And Marx and Engels saw that this could only be a new kind of class dictatorship, one that will open up totally new possibilities for all of humanity. It will be the first dictatorship of the propertyless majority, those whose own liberation requires the abolition of every form of oppression and exploitation on the face of the earth. That's the process the last class to rule in history will set in motion. For the first time, a new ruling class will not institute a new form of class exploitation. Rather, it will, step by step, eliminate all exploitation. The dictatorship of the proletariat itself will wither away as classes and the institutions of class society, including the family and state, do so—and as the new communist society comes into being.

This understanding placed socialism on a scientific basis for the first time. The dictatorship of the proletariat is the first and only class dictatorship that is conscious of why it arises, what it must do, and how it and all politics will wither away and disappear from the face of the earth.

"What the bourgeoisie, therefore, produces, above all, is its own gravediggers. Its fall and the victory of the proletariat are equally inevitable." That's what Marx and Engels said was the meaning of the struggle of this new class of hereditary proletarians. They said it in the *Communist Manifesto*, a summary of this new world view, the conscious world view of a class, the proletariat.

History is on our side

In the SWP Leadership School, we spent several days going over the *Manifesto*, paragraph by paragraph. You don't have time to do that normally. But sometime just take a paragraph, or sentence, from the *Manifesto* and turn it over in your mind from the point of view of your class and your experience as class conscious workers.

One of the most important points we discussed was that the "theoretical conclusions of the Communists are in no way based on ideas or principles that have been invented, or discovered, by this or that would-be universal reformer."

The theoretical conclusions the Communists express are, "in general terms, actual relations springing from an existing class struggle, from a historical movement going on under our very eyes."

"The Communists, therefore, are on the one hand, practically, the most advanced and resolute section of the working-class parties of every country, that section which pushes forward all others; on the other hand, theoretically, they have over the great mass of the proletariat the advantage of clearly understanding the *line of march*, the *conditions*, and the *ultimate general* results of the proletarian movement."

Marxists "are distinguished by the fact" that in working class struggles in any country "they point out and bring to the front the common interests of the entire proletariat, independent of all nationality." And no matter what stage the working class movement is at, always and everywhere they express the revolutionary interests of the working class as a whole and represent its future interests as they fight in the present.

Marxism includes the lessons of the struggle of the working class, of its defeats, of its victories, of the bloodshed and horror it has had to endure—to learn from the past, so the errors do not have to be repeated and the blood was not shed in vain.

Communists "have no interests separate and apart from those of the proletariat as a whole." Therefore, "they do not set up any sectarian [or separate] principles of their own, by which to shape or mold the proletarian movement." Understanding that is understanding the source of the power of Marxism. You do not bring a message to the working-class movement; you see and understand the living movement as it exists; you can thus see its road forward, which is nothing other than the inevitable strategic line of march of our class.

Marx and Engels, looking at the present as history, said over and over again that the victory of the proletariat is inevitable. We do not invent this for reassurance; we discover this fact through participating in the class struggle, its twists and turns and complications, confronting obstacles and new complications that continually arise. Seeing this fact clearly and fully, and acting upon it, we are in the vanguard of the first class in history whose development requires it to change the world and to do so consciously. Thinking and doing are seen in their revolutionary unity for the first time. We simply shine a flashlight down the road our class must take; we don't make a single thing up.

I thought of this while I read the *Militant* [August 8 issue] this week. At least four times, four different people, in four different articles sent the message of the inevitable triumph of the proletariat to their class and to the enemy class.

One was the page 4 interview with John Wood, the 19-year-old comrade from Baltimore who told Carter to take his registration and stuff it. At the end of the interview he said he was very optimistic, because "history is on our side."

Comrade Fidel, on July 26, quoted on page 5, explained the same thing when he said that the socialist road is the only road for every country. There is no other road than the socialist revolution, not because he wills it, but "by the imperative of history."

A few days before, an international representative of the United Auto Workers, Robert Lopez, gave a wonderful speech on Nicaragua in Detroit (that says a lot about Nicaragua and a little something about the union movement). It's on page 6.

He spoke about U.S. policy in Latin America, and pointed out, "it is a desperate policy by madmen, who are boxed in by history."

And right down below that article was one concerning the July 26 rally in New York where Raul Roa said those who wish to turn back the clock are "on the wrong side of history."

They all have one thing in common. They know, or at least sense, where history is going, and they draw their greatest strength from that. Their strength does not lie in their hope, their strength is not primarily their individual strength, their strength comes from the knowledge that they are marching forward with humanity. They know this and understand it. And that understanding is the greatest motivation to devote yourself to becoming a Bolshevik fighter.

Many of us join our movement because we reject the horrors of capitalism and want to see a more just, humane, and rational society. But we don't become Marxists, we don't become revolutionary socialists, we don't become conscious worker-Bolsheviks until we understand this necessary and inevitable line of march in our bones, and can transmit that fact. That is the real communist, Marxist message to fellow workers.

Thus sectarian schemes are the opposite of Marxism. An example of the sectarian approach would be, in face of the beginning socialist revolution in Grenada, to lament the fact that it didn't occur in a bigger country like Brazil, because that was the way you thought things *ought* to develop. No one who thinks like that should be able to hold up their heads in the workers' movement.

Another example would be to turn away from the revolution in Nicaragua, and not throw yourself into it, because the form of the government at this stage is not the form that you had in mind, when you were thinking about what the next revolution should be like in Latin America.

Proletarian internationalism

As part of this fundamental materialist class outlook, Marx and Engels emphasized internationalism. We often talk about learning from the Russians and we often talk about Americanizing our movement. And both things can be good. The Russians were the first to successfully lead the workers to power and consciously tried to develop the strategy to extend their victory. And they put it in writing. And they organized a force to implement it. And we have to Americanize our movement in certain ways, as Engels explained when he gave the German-American comrades hell for not learning English. One way to Americanize the movement is to learn Spanish so we can communicate with a lot of American workers.

But the key thing is not to Americanize our party, or simply to learn from the Russians. The key thing is to *internationalize* our party, because our class is international. It is not national. That is the lesson we learn from Marx and Engels that is decisive for the world revolution.

They drew a very important conclusion from this fact. Any Marxist in any country has to have the goal in mind of building a world party. A worldwide communist, Marxist party. Although at the time the *Communist Manifesto* was written, the communist movement was relatively few people, holding small meetings, with few links with the industrial workers, facing all kinds of problems, the *Manifesto* proudly proclaimed and insisted it was an international manifesto, and announced the languages it would be translated into for the workers of the world.

As Fidel says, any national egoism, any chauvinism, any idea you can finish the construction of socialism in any country before you have world socialism, and thus, feed, clothe, and advance "the great majority of humanity" is alien to Marxism.

Liberation of oppressed nations

Another thing that Marx and Engels gave us was an understanding of the interpenetration of the class struggle with the fight of the oppressed nations for liberation. Lenin's slogan, "Workers and oppressed nations of the world unite" was new, the idea was not. This idea came into its own in a new way in the imperialist epoch with the victory of the Russian revolution and the risings of the colonial peoples. This concept was not just an idea the SWP developed in the 60s in relation to the oppressed nationalities in the U.S. either. It is a fundamental tenet of Marxism. It tells the oppressed peoples, "We champion your just demands and your battles. We welcome your fighters to our ranks. Your battle is ours, our battle is yours."

Marxism teaches us to see all phenomena in

class terms. As the class struggle intensifies, this becomes more and more important to understand. Words like democracy, freedom, war, responsibility, fairness, equality, don't have any meaning unless they're given a class context.

Democracy for what layer or class?

Freedom for whom to do what to whom?

War by whom for what goals?

Equality for whom? By what road?

Fairness for what class?

Responsibility? How many times have you been told to be responsible? To which class? You have to say, "To which class, mom?" That's a difference between children growing up in Cuba today and children who grow up in the United States. We didn't know what question to ask when we were told to be responsible. We learned a little later than Cuban children do, but we learned.

Our heritage

The revolutionary strategy and tactics that are our heritage, the heritage of the workers of the world, were built around what Marx and Engels learned and generalized from the struggles of the working class. Thus they discovered the laws of motion of capitalism and their meaning for our class. That's what they gave us.

When you read Lenin, you will discover something that may seem surprising. Lenin is filled with quotations from Marx and Engels. Lenin fought to preserve the lessons learned by Marx and Engels against all those in the socialist movement who turned away from the revolutionary conclusions of these lessons, and who tried to cover up what Marx and Engels said and wrote. In so doing, in his study of Marx and Engels, he discovered that Marxism developed through the struggles of the proletariat in big revolutions, in uprisings, in the attempts by the proletariat to establish its dictatorship.

Fidel Castro explained years ago that the Cuban revolutionists, in the course of their struggle, became Marxist-Leninists; that they had to go back to the scientific foundations of socialism laid by the founders of our movement.

This is the common ground on which all genuine proletarian revolutionists meet, whatever different paths we take to get there. All proletarian revolutionists should be willing to be judged by this criterion: how well are they carrying out the job of our class, discovered by Marx and Engels and developed by Lenin and the team around him, of preparing for, taking, and using proletarian state power, nationally and internationally.

The questions of today were worked on, and basic strategic guidelines for how to approach them were developed initially by Marx and Engels. Questions such as alliances; workers' and farmers' governments; the national question; women's rights; the necessity of the independent organization of the proletariat; workers' newspapers; how to agitate; when and how to carry out guerrilla war; how to do barricades fighting; how to lead a "people's revolution" forward; how to smash the state; the difference between the lumpen, which the ruling class use, and so-called "hoodlums," the young workers who are the most combative part of our class; international collaboration; and the need for an international party. Marx and Engels taught us a lot on these things, before Lenin came around, before Trotsky continued and added to Leninism, let alone before we came along.

For example, we have faced plant closings in the recent period. When they close down your plant, one of the ideas that often comes up is that the workers should get together and buy the plant. That idea came up over a century ago. Marx and Engels thought through that proposal, the fallacies involved in it, how to explain it clearly, and deal with it. Their answer remains correct today.

The capitalists are blaming imports and foreign workers for the terrible problems they themselves impose on us today. The same thing happened over a hundred years ago. The answer to this capitalist argument was given way back then.

Or, take the fact that inflation is killing us. Taxes are killing us. We've got to have cheap government. That was one of the lessons of the Paris Commune. You get cheap government when you get rid of most government. And only a workers' regime can accomplish that.

What about affirmative action?

Marx wrote in 1875, in his criticism of the unification program of German socialism, an exposure of bourgeois "equality" that underlies our entire concept of affirmative action. He criticized the German party for not explaining that workers who have unequal beginnings, if treated equally, will inevitably suffer deepening inequality. We must not just approach workers as workers, Marx said, but as differentiated by other factors that give "unequal individual endowment." And we must point out that it will be necessary to compensate for this not only under capitalism but under a workers' government "as it emerges from capitalist society" for a transitional period.

When we debated the question of affirmative action a few years ago, there was an idea that while we were sure this was absolutely correct today, it was a new-fangled notion not to be found in Marx. That was simply false. Actually, we were rediscovering late in the game the revolutionary application of a basic Marxist concept. If I remember correctly, I don't think we ever once quoted Marx on this during the entire time we argued this question internally, or have been writing about in the *Militant*.

It is important to rediscover the heritage of our movement. The Marxist tendency is distinguished from all others in the workers' movement by the fact that it represents the continuity of the lessons of the movement. Any retreat from these lessons leads toward defeats for the working class. And it is important to rediscover it along with those who are acting as revolutionists on a world scale.

Learning Marxism

The students at Sandstone learned Spanish. One good reason for doing this is that we're internationalists. Spanish is important for us in collaborating with revolutionists in Central America and the Caribbean, a focal point of the international class struggle. Since we didn't have a TV at the school, we listened to Radio Havana a lot. And we had to learn Spanish to know what Radio Havana was saying.

Another good reason to learn Spanish is so we can communicate with the large Spanish-speaking section of the American working class. This is necessary to lead the revolution in this country. One of the most important projects we can set ourselves in the party is to advance the determination of the membership to learn Spanish.

We bear all the scars of our education and miseducation through the imperialist attitudes the ruling class fosters in us. Americans are taught that the whole world will listen to you if you speak English. We're told the whole world seeks the American dollar, the whole world will doff their caps when we pass. Americans are raised with the idea that if they jabber a minority language at the world, everyone will, or ought to, understand them. We're all raised with those deep prejudices, and we should never underestimate them.

I was convinced of something else by this leadership school. I was convinced that the only people qualified to really learn Marxism are the cadres of the revolutionary workers' movement. No one else can learn it, no one else will learn it.

The comrades at the school were the same kind of people as those in this room. They worked in the same plants. They joined the same kind of party. They have the same backgrounds as you have. They discovered their unsuspected capacities to absorb, learn, and relearn Marxism.

Marxism will never be learned in isolation from the working-class movement. It never has been. There is no exception to this rule. Science isolated from the working class can develop *tools* that are useful to Marxism, but Marxism could only come out of the movement whose struggle it reflects and generalizes, the working-class movement. Petty bourgeois prejudice would have you believe just the opposite. There are "Marxists" like Herbert Marcuse and other "Western Marxists" who reject the necessary connection between the rise of the industrial proletariat, its interests and its development, and the development of social theory and political strategy. They spin their theories abstracted from and in isolation from (and more and more in opposition to) the forward movement of the working class.

But workers, conscious of themselves, conscious of their class position, knowing where they're heading, are uniquely qualified to study, learn, and add to the Marxist heritage. This is the *only* way of enriching the Marxist heritage.

We reached the stage in our studies when the comrades got more and more furious with many of the introductions to the works of the great Marxists, and with the various biographers of Marx and Engels. To their great surprise, they discovered they knew more about Marxism than authors of the many "introductions" to Marx and Engels who write the critiques, write the biographies—and who literally know nothing about Marxism. Marxism is being learned by revolutionary workers in the schools of the mines, the mills, the factories, the jungles, and the cities of Central America and the Caribbean. They are learning, revitalizing and using Marxism today. That's how we're doing it, too, here in the United States and in the other sections and sympathizing organizations of the Fourth International. And that's who we want to do it with.

A world Marxist movement

The most important single organizational conclusion of Marxism is the need for a world party, a world Marxist movement. Without that the world revolution can take certain steps forward, with great pain and many losses, but cannot sweep to victory. This conclusion has been at the heart of Marxism from its inception. All the great Marxists tried to build such a world party. Marx and Engels addressed the *Communist Manifesto* to the workers of the world. They organized the First International—a small, vanguard, originally very politically heterogeneous group—that tried to lay the groundwork for the first international assault on capital by the workers. In so doing they helped to deal a mortal blow to pre-Marxian petty-bourgeois socialism, which was a fundamental problem in the workers movement.

After the defeat of the Paris Commune, the First International was no longer viable as an organization. Marx and Engels turned to helping as best they could the European movement, the Russian movement, and the American movement.

When the Second International was formed in 1889, it marked a new stage in the level of organization of the proletariat. The first big independent mass proletarian parties developed in much of Europe. They considered themselves Marxist parties. But this evolution had another side to it. There was an erosion of the revolutionary and internationalist goals, spirit, and Marxist program of these parties. This reached its fruition in the debacle of World War I, when the leaders of most socialist parties in the Second International supported "their" bourgeoisies in the imperialist slaughter, setting workers of each nation against each other in the service of capital.

But out of the leadership of the Russian party of the Second International, a leadership that *was* Marxist, the Bolsheviks, emerged—and led the Russian revolution. That opened up the third great attempt to build an international revolutionary workers' movement, along the lines laid down by the *Communist Manifesto*. This third attempt began, as Lenin pointed out, in 1918 with the first determined steps of revolutionists around the world to build Marxist parties like the Bolshevik party. That, Lenin says, was the new international. These new parties came together in 1919 to set up the Communist International. This new international, unlike the First and Second, operated in a world where socialist revolution had been proven possible, where the workers in one country had a revolutionary leadership and held state power. That changed a lot of the rules. That state power was an invaluable asset. The Communist International fought to maintain that state power, and to use it to help extend the world revolution. The international set as its goal the wider and wider unification of soviet socialist republics established through the advance of the world revolution.

The Communist International was formed as Communist parties were organized around the world. The colonial masses were drawn into the Marxist movement in large numbers for the first time. The Communist International was a real international in that sense. The lessons of the Russian revolution and the writings of its revolutionary leaders were made available to million and millions, and that can never be taken away.

Once again, however, contradictory aspects appeared in the new international. The Communist International itself declined and degenerated. "Peaceful coexistence" with the imperialists—which, as Lenin and Trotsky had used the term, was a way of gaining time to advance the world revolution—was transformed by the rising Soviet bureaucracy into its opposite: seeking accommodation with imperialism *against* the world revolution. This was theorized by Stalin and Bukharin and given the name "socialism in one country." It's what is meant by "detente" today by Stalin's heirs in Moscow and Peking.

The world proletariat suffered grievous defeats under this policy, leading to the second great imperialist slaughter. Already dead as a revolutionary instrument, the Third International was formally buried by Stalin in 1943 as a favor to

Franklin Delano Roosevelt.

But the followers of Lenin, those who fought to maintain the revolutionary continuity of Marxism against the Stalinist degeneration, were able to hold together nuclei of Bolshevik-Leninist parties based on the acquisitions and additions to Marxism of the first four Congresses of the Communist International. Under Trotsky's leadership they formed an international current in 1928, and in 1938 formed the Fourth International. The Fourth International wasn't a massive international based on a victorious revolution like the Third. It wasn't an international based on mass parties, like the Second. It has no mass parties. It was a small nucleus, forced to swim against the stream, that maintained and developed the Marxist program by participation in the class struggle as best it could, an irreplaceable task and contribution. And Trotsky bore the greatest single responsibility for achieving that. This nucleus looked forward to building a world party, based on mass parties that led masses in combat. It thought that a mighty new revolutionary wave emerging from the horror of the Second World War would be the basis for rebuilding the Marxist movement.

But World War II led to contradictory results. The victory of the Soviet Union against German imperialism was a great victory for the workers everywhere, but it had the contradictory side effect of refurbishing Stalinism's reputation. Stalinist parties continued to dominate the movement in much of Europe. The Stalinists betrayed the revolution in Italy, France, and Greece, setting back the working class in all of Europe. The extension of the world revolution in Yugoslavia, China, and Eastern Europe was marred by their Stalinist leaderships, which gravely deformed them and limited their ability to give an impulse and leadership to the spread of the world revolution.

The fifties and sixties did not bring the extension of the East European workers' revolutions into Western Europe. Thanks to the Stalinist betrayal, world capitalism was given a breathing space to recover and then launch an offensive based on a massive economic expansion on a world scale.

The extension of the revolution, even though gravely deformed, following World War II, led nevertheless to the breakup of the Stalinist monolith. The bureaucratic castes in China and in Yugoslavia had their own interests to defend as against the Kremlin. And the beginnings of the political revolution appeared in Eastern Europe—East Germany in 1953, and Poland and Hungary in 1956.

Historic breakthrough

But in Cuba, in the middle of the capitalist expansion, an entirely new phenomenon appeared—a revolutionary leadership of non-Stalinist origin led a genuinely popular revolution, and then led the workers to state power. They linked the Cuban revolution with the existing workers' states, which, regardless of their degeneration, had not been overthrown by capitalist counterrevolution. In the process, through their experiences and study the Cuban revolutionaries became Marxists, and this opened a new period for the world revolution.

When Che Guevara was murdered in 1967, we put out a book of his speeches. The younger leaders in the SWP at that time were deeply affected by the murder of Che, as we had been by that of Malcolm X. These were our first great losses of that kind. Maybe it was our first real understanding of what we were involved in. Partly for this reason Joe Hansen wrote an introduction to *Che Guevara Speaks,* explaining Che's and Fidel's historical significance. Giving the considered judgment of the Socialist Workers Party after nine years of the Cuban revolution, he said:

> Something bigger even than Che is involved—the Cuban Revolution and its contribution toward solving the most crucial single problem facing humanity: the construction of a leadership capable of guiding the way out of an economic order reeking in every pore with corruption, filth and blood.
>
> Like many in previous generations, the young people who led the Cuban Revolution saw the poverty, the hunger, the abysmal conditions of life, the oppression, making a hell of their country. They also saw how senseless this was and how modern industry and science could change it from top to bottom. Like previous generations they found the contrast between what is and what could be absolutely intolerable. And like many who had preceded them, they saw that, in view of the role of the oligarchy and its imperialist backers, revolu-

tion offered the only possible way of ending the insufferable present and opening up a new perspective.

But unlike the majority of those in the immediately preceding decades, they depended on their own judgment, their own initiative and their own independent efforts to achieve what they sought. They did not fall into either of two very common traps. They did not rely for leadership on the so-called progressive sector of the national bourgeoisie of their own country or on the ossified bureaucracy running the Communist party.

This was one of the most significant aspects of the Cuban Revolution. It provided the main key to success, for it made it possible to outflank the Communist party, which had stood as the major obstacle to a successful revolution in Cuba since the establishment of the Blas Roca leadership with its policy of "peaceful coexistence" and even collaboration with the Batista dictatorship and the Roosevelt administration.

To Che Guevara, along with Fidel Castro, belongs the credit for hewing to this course of action no matter what the consequences. These leaders and the team they built appeared on the scene, evidently as forerunners of a great new development in world politics—the rise of a generation of revolutionary fighters disinclined to accept either Moscow or Peking or any similar center as a kind of Vatican that in practice serves to stultify both revolutionary theory and practice.

Thus from a political point of view, the major interest in Che Guevara's development is the line of thought and action that enabled him to grow from a petty-bourgeois rebel into an effective leader, committed to the socialist goal, whose outlook converged more and more with the classical revolutionary Marxist tradition that stood behind the October 1917 Russian Revolution.

While this introduction was one of the most clear and concise statements of the party's evaluation of the caliber of the Castro leadership, Joe really wasn't breaking any new ground. We had been following the development of the Cuban team from the outset, as you know from reading Joe's book [*Dynamics of the Cuban Revolution*, Pathfinder Press].

In one of Joe's articles, written in 1965, he explained the significance of the reorganization of the Cuban party that year and the change of its name from the United Party of the Socialist Revolution to the Cuban Communist Party. Joe explained that "this is not a reedition of the old Communist Party of Stalinist days" in Cuba. He explained how the original Castro team used the 1965 reorganization to consolidate its position in the unified party that had been formed three years earlier with the fusion of the Stalinist Communist Party and the July 26 Movement.

"The overall balance of the reorganization and renaming of the party," Joe said, "further emphasizes its independence from the old Stalinist machine, its identity with the activists who carried out the Cuban revolution, and its commitment to the ideology of revolutionary Marxism."

What Joe had to say about the Cuban team in 1965 and 1967 is even more true today.

From the beginning, the Cubans have attempted to extend their revolution. Following the defeats of the guerrilla groupings in Latin America, there was a period of time when we were not so sure what was happening in Cuba. If we had followed it more closely, we would have known, because it wasn't any secret. The Cubans were talking about it and writing about it.

We were conscious of Cuba's unceasing internationalist solidarity with Vietnam and attitude to U.S. imperialism, contrasting it in our press to the grudging aid and political betrayals by Moscow and Peking in their pursuit of a deal with Washington. But for several years we stopped following closely other developments in Cuba, and we stopped going down to Cuba nearly as much as we should have.

During these years, some comrades decided that a fundamental right turn was going on. Perhaps the tremendous problems the Cubans faced were causing a degeneration—not just a dangerous development of rightist bureaucratic elements, but a process that reached right into the central leadership. Perhaps the failure of the guerrilla war efforts and the effects of more than a decade of the Yankee blockade had demoralized the Cuban leaders, turning them to more stable and safer pursuits.

Joe always resisted those who claimed to perceive a fundamental right turn by the Castro leadership. He thought something different was going on. In an article he wrote in 1970, Joe explained that the Cubans were engaged in "a pause for reflection" over the failure of the guerrilla *strategy.* He came back to the term in his introduction to *Dynamics of the Cuban Revolution* eight years later, saying that the Cubans had used the pause for "consideration of possible alternatives." During that period, Joe said, "the Cuban leaders had to reassess priorities and set more modest goals" in face of the possibilities on a world scale.

The Cubans' unflagging stand with Vietnam throughout the final five years of the war was a sign that they were far from giving up on the extension of the world revolution.

This became obvious with the change in the world balance of forces marked by the 1975 defeat for Washington in Vietnam. The Cubans responded to the new opportunities made possible by this weakening of U.S. imperialism by acting as revolutionists, as proletarian internationalists. And, as Joe put it, "One of the by-products of Cuba's fresh leap into world prominence has been a renewal of interest in the nature of the Cuban revolution, in the political character of its leadership. . . . "

From 1975 on, only the willfully ignorant could miss what was happening. There was a new initiative by the Cubans that settled in life the question of which direction they were going. The Cubans sized up the relationship of forces following the U.S. defeat in Vietnam and went to Africa to fight the South African invasion of Angola and, later, the imperialist-backed attack on the Ethiopian revolution by Somalia. They also showed they understood the limits of the use of troops—they never tried to substitute their troops for the self-conscious action of the African toilers themselves. They had no crude concept of "exporting" revolution on the point of a bayonet.

And by the end of the 1970s and opening of the 1980s, the Cubans were throwing everything they had behind the extension of the revolution in Central America, and in support of the Grenadian revolution. Their course is clear. The Cubans have learned from experience, have deepened their Marxist understanding, and have corrected errors. But they have not changed their basic revolutionary course.

A process of political growth

The Cuban leaders have become more materialist, more Marxist. They believe that history is on their side, and that the socialist revolution is inevitable. Not only is it inevitable, but the last twenty years have convinced them that there is no other road forward for any country in the world. And they say so.

In his July 26 speech this year, Castro singled out Cuba, Nicaragua, and Grenada as the three countries in Latin America "free . . . of imperialism." He expressed his gratitude to Panama, Jamaica, and Mexico for maintaining diplomatic and trade relations with Cuba in the face of imperialist pressure. "But three of us," he said, "have shaken the yoke of imperialism in the last 20 years in a radical way, once and for all and it is a historical imperative that one day we'll all be free. . . . all the peoples of Latin America and the Caribbean."

Drawing on defeats as well as victories, Castro said, "The Guatemalan experience, the Salvadoran experience, the Chilean experience, the Bolivian experience, what have they taught us? That there is only one path: revolution! That there is only one way: revolutionary armed struggle!"

The Cubans have learned the dead-end of what Marx and Engels described as parliamentary cretinism. Any idea that the workers can establish socialism through capitalist elections and parliaments, without smashing the old state and replacing it with a workers' state, is a fake and a fraud.

"The oligarchy, reaction and imperialism use all these so-called constitutional mechanisms, the so-called representative democracy, to deceive the peoples," Fidel told the July 26 crowd. "Even when the overwhelming majority of people through the democratic, or so-called democratic mechanisms, vote against a reactionary government and in favor of a progressive government, or even a democratic government, there's a coup d'etat. Like in Chile, in Bolivia. And the peoples learned their lessons and saw that there was only one road to liberation: that of Cuba, that of Grenada, that of Nicaragua. There is no other formula."

Che Guevara in 1967 coined the slogan, "Either

socialist revolution or a caricature of revolution." But then, he was speaking only of the Latin American continent. That has changed. In speech after speech, the Cubans have explained the necessity of socialist revolution throughout the world.

Castro reiterated something else on July 26th that had been reconfirmed in action in Nicaragua. He pointed to the decisive role of the organization and the struggle in the cities, in the proletarian centers.

The Cubans have become *more* proletarian, as well as *more* internationalist. They have been taught by the workers, as they've explained. The same thing happened to the Cuban leadership as happened to Farrell Dobbs in the Minneapolis Teamsters struggle. Farrell expressed it this way in the dedication of the first of the Teamsters books: "To the men and women who gave me unshakable confidence in the working class, the rank and file of General Drivers Local 574." That's what the Cubans have been taught by the workers of the world. Everyone who remains a revolutionist is taught this at some time.

Deepening revolution in Cuba

The problems the Castroists are grappling with in Cuba are many of the same ones the Bolsheviks faced—the alliance with the peasantry, which no leadership has ever handled better than the Cubans; the extension of education to the workers and peasants as a precondition for real workers democracy; extension of health care to the masses; promoting equality; ending the domestic slavery of women; etc.

We too will face these problems, although in the different context created by an advanced capitalist economy. For example, the question of the alliance with the farmers. Serious workers will ask us someday, well, if you win, how are you going to feed this whole population? Because they will know that very rapidly, unless you have an alliance with the farmers, the cities will starve. As Liam James explained last night, it's those kind of problems that make the insurrection look easy.

How to fight bureaucratism? Lenin explained that bureaucratism cannot be prevented short of a victory of world socialism. Trotsky repeated that truth. But how can it be limited, contained, and held in check so that it does not become dominant over the workers? The main way is to go to the mass of the toilers, educating and mobilizing them, time after time, around the real revolutionary challenges that will enable the workers to overcome the problems and institutionalize their advances. Of course, nothing else has had the impact of the extension of the socialist revolution into Nicaragua and Grenada on the revolutionary mobilization of the Cuban masses, and this has dealt the biggest blow yet to bureaucratic tendencies.

The political level of the Cuban working class is the highest in the world. For two decades the workers have been mobilized and educated around all the great questions before the world revolution and the Cuban revolution, from land reform to the meaning of the Vietnamese revolution, from the literacy and education drives to the importance of beating back South Africa in Angola, from learning to cope with the U.S. blockade to the importance of the fact that Cuba is "no longer alone" in the Americas, from the need for Cuba to be internationalist to the need to study Marx, Engels, and Lenin.

When Fidel speaks, he does not do it primarily for the benefit of either opponents or enemies abroad. He doesn't speak for intellectuals interested in analyzing his thoughts. He doesn't speak for a privileged few that are educated enough to understand. He deals with the most fundamental perspectives of the world revolution, talking directly with the Cuban workers, and increasingly, the workers of the world.

The political level of the Cuban workers was expressed in the March of the Fighting People. Literally half the island came out to celebrate the breaking of twenty years of isolation in the Americas, to defy imperialism, and to let both imperialism and the toiling masses elsewhere know that Cuba stands behind Nicaragua, Grenada, and the developing socialist revolution in the region. That's after twenty years of unrelenting imperialist attack, blockade, and pressure.

The Cubans have done pretty good on racism at home, and identification with the African masses. They are doing very well in the fight for women's rights. The scientific understanding of women's liberation and the roots of women's oppression in class society is more advanced in Cuba today than it was in the Soviet Union in the period of

Lenin and Trotsky. Most importantly, the Cuban women and the Cuban leadership, are grappling with this question in real life as it is not being done anywhere in the world.

There's a wonderful book called *Children of the Revolution* by Jonathan Kozol, who went to Cuba to study their education system. The achievements of the Cubans in this field are amazing. Remember, Lenin pointed out that real "workers' management" could only be achieved in a constant battle to overcome the inherited lack of education of the Russian masses. The imperialist invasions and civil war cut that short in the Soviet Union. The Cubans are making big strides toward overcoming their inherited backwardness.

Kozol went to a high school that was built in the early seventies. It was the first of the schools "out in the country," where the students got away from their families, away from the city in a work-study program. The school was to be named for Che Guevara. But the students and teachers, moved by the 1970 antiwar upsurge in the United States, decided to name it for the American antiwar fighters, who gave them a whole new view of the United States. They named it, "School of the Martyrs of Kent."

Kozol describes his discussions with a group of students. He debates with them, and their views blow his mind. He knows he's seeing the future, not the past. They can't convince him that they actually believe that a person's principles, what you live for—humanity as a whole—are more important than your individual life. And the Cuban students can't understand how he doesn't see that, or why they can't convince him that freedom is most fundamentally defined as freedom from exploitation.

Kozol asked them what message they would like to send to their fellow junior high schools in the United States. They got together, thought about it, and said: "Tell them, please, that we support them in their fight against their rulers—whoever they are—the corporations or the CIA. We do not suggest, however, that they think about the use of weapons. They cannot use weapons because of their situation and their age. We would advise them first to read more books about important struggles like Moncada. We would advise them to read speeches of Fidel and also, of course, to read the works of Che . . . We would advise them also to read books by Marx and Engels . . ." That was the message from Cuba's junior high school students!

Cuba and world politics

Two questions often raised by Marxists are whether the Cuban leadership has a wrong analysis of the political position concerning the United States and the Soviet Union, which are the two major powers of the world. The Cuban leadership has made a lot of mistakes, and they themselves will explain many of them to you. But their view of the United States is not their problem.

They see that the United States is a powerful imperialist bastion that has to have a socialist revolution. They saw the development of the antiwar movement during the Vietnam War as not only important for Vietnam, but also for the United States. They are convinced, as they have been from day one of the revolution, that the Black struggle is the vanguard of the American proletarian movement, and they never stop covering it in their press. They look forward to the development of the class struggle in the United States and the development of the leadership of the American working class, which will lead the historically decisive overthrow of U.S. capitalism. Building that leadership is not their problem, it's our problem. The problem is not understanding the nature of the United States; it's *doing* something about it.

Concerning the Soviet Union. Our understanding of the development of the bureaucratic caste in the world's first workers' state and of the role of Stalinism is one of the most fundamental legacies we have in our arsenal of Marxism. Trotsky developed a scientific understanding of the contradictory results of the evolution of the Soviet Union. On the one side, the bureaucratic counterrevolution headed by Stalin failed to overturn the fundamental gains the workers made in the October revolution. Instead, there is an objective tendency for the Soviet property forms to spread to new workers' states through socialist revolutions. On the other side, however, the counterrevolutionary bureaucratic caste turned the teachings of Lenin into their opposite, which has created a massive obstacle to the advance of the revolution in the USSR and throughout the world. Lenin's proletarian internationalism and revolutionary program for the world was transformed into its opposite, the "second wave of Menshevism," with all its devastating effects on the proletariat.

This understanding is an important test that we have passed. But there's another test, the test of practice. It is a higher test. The Cubans did rather well in dealing with the 1962 missile crisis, where the government of the Soviet Union joined with Washington to totally exclude the Cubans from the resolution of big questions affecting Cuba's sovereignty and security. The Cubans did rather well with the Escalante affair—their first direct experience with Stalinist bureaucratism in post revolutionary Cuba. They have had to grapple with the problem of the "faint-hearted," who turn away from internationalism to seek accommodation with imperialism. During the 1968 Czechoslovakia events, they took the wrong political position, in our opinion. But Castro's speech at the time had another side to it—the beginnings of a Marxist understanding of bureaucracy and the danger it represents to the revolution.

During the Vietnam War the Cubans offered to fight and die for Vietnam. They called on the workers of the world, and all the workers' states, to join in a united front to make Vietnam an inviolable territory of the socialist world. The Cuban masses understood that the best way to help Vietnam was to create "two, three, many Vietnams." And they tried to do that, to extend the revolution.

"Everything we have is yours," they said to Vietnam. That's what Moscow and Peking should have said too, but didn't, as the Cubans found ways and means to point out.

Now the Cubans are campaigning for aid to Nicaragua. Last year Fidel called upon the industrially advanced countries of the world, the big countries, the imperialist countries, the colonial countries, the progressive countries, the socialist countries—to have a contest to see who could give more aid to Nicaragua, to emulate Cuba in pouring in the aid.

On July 19 this year, speaking in Managua, Fidel indicated he was disappointed in the results of this emulation campaign.

In considering this question, we have to note that Cuba has managed to survive in this world as a revolutionary workers' government for twenty years. They have managed to survive because of aid from the Soviet Union. Fidel put it this way on July 26: "The Soviet worker who grows wheat in the Ukraine or extracts oil in Siberia and ships it to the ports and from the ports to Cuba has helped us tremendously. So have the technicians from the Soviet Union and other socialist countries, and the arms we've received to defend ourselves so that we can today feel secure and not be afraid of anyone—including Reagan or King Kong, if he were president of the United States."

The Cubans have used their revolutionary government for twenty years to fight to extend the world socialist revolution. This is the most decisive difference between their policy and that of Stalinism, its polar opposite and mortal enemy.

Building the world party of revolution

Most important of all, Fidel knows how to listen and learn. This is an ability that must be cultivated by those who consider themselves part of the Marxist vanguard. This is a real test for proletarian revolutionists, and there's never been a proletarian revolutionist who hasn't had the ability to listen and learn. There's never been a person worth a damn in the plants, the unions, or the mass organizations who can't listen and learn.

Fidel means it when he says the Cubans are going to learn from Nicaragua. They're going to learn about how workers' control is being used in Nicaragua. He says they're going to learn about the mass organizations, about the neighborhood Sandinista Defense Committees and unions that arose in Nicaragua in a different way than in Cuba. They are going to learn from Nicaragua's experience if they succeed in drawing the broad masses into governing the country as the revolution moves forward and the country is rebuilt.

Fidel doesn't approach the new features that emerged out of the Nicaraguan struggle defending preconceived schemas—"That wasn't how I thought it would happen." And like Fidel, we have to be able to listen and learn, and be ready to change on the basis of what we learn.

After his visit, Nicaraguans said, "Fidel is a Sandinista." We said the Nicaraguans are Fidelistas. Grenadians are Sandinistas. Cubans are Grenadians. The truth of the matter is they are Marxists and aspire to be better ones as they act as revolutionaries. They are a revolutionary Marxist current, a proletarian current, living and struggling to extend the socialist revolution today. We judge them by their actions primarily, as we expect to be judged.

The existence of this current, and the new steps forward it is making today, are decisive, as Joe Hansen said, in overcoming the single most important question facing humanity—the crisis of proletarian leadership.

This is not just a question for us in North America, in the United States and Canada. It is not just a question of concern only to the Americas. It cannot be reduced to that. This is a question of the leadership of the proletariat of the world.

The Fourth International was founded to work toward overcoming the crisis of leadership of the proletariat. As we said at the time of the 1963 reunification, "*The Trotskyist movement has no interests separate and apart from the long-range ones of the world proletariat.* It is not interested in constructing an 'organization' simply for its own sake or as a mere pressure group. The organization it seeks to build is a definite means to a definite end—the victory of the proletariat on a world scale."

The nucleus that was put together to form the Fourth International seeks to join with revolutionary currents that are bound to rise in the course of the class struggle.

But the Fourth International has suffered, for objective causes, from what, for lack of a better term, I'll call a semi-sectarian existence. Its sections have been relatively small formations, in most countries isolated from their class in day-to-day life, in a period when the working class in many countries was not the main actor on the political stage.

Since 1968 in certain countries in Europe, and since the mid-1970s throughout the imperialist countries, including the United States, we have seen a new radicalization of the working class. In the semicolonial countries, too, the proletariat has moved to the fore. This is enabling our forces to move out of our isolation and into the industrial proletariat. These changes have also affected the Castroist current, and are one factor in the convergence between this current and ourselves. Now we see the Cuban revolution being extended in Central America and the Caribbean, at the same time the radicalization of the proletariat on a world scale is deepening.

At the World Congress of the Fourth International in November 1979, we joined with a majority of comrades in arguing for the entire international making a decisive turn into industry. The only possible conclusion that can be drawn from the changes in the objective situation on a world scale is that our comrades everywhere must go into the mines, mills, and factories now. On this proposition, we were successful, and a majority voted to carry out this turn.

But on the other side of the new reality, we failed. We fought at the Congress to get the comrades to realize that not only were the workers and peasants in the saddle in Nicaragua, but that the FSLN was a revolutionary leadership and part of a revolutionary current. It is a leadership we must seek to collaborate with as fellow Marxists, who've already proven themselves. We even made an attempt to get the discussion going on the revolutionary developments in Grenada.

But on this crucial question, we failed to gain the understanding of a majority of comrades. Now we have to go forward. The turn must be carried out and deepened by all sections of the Fourth International. Without the turn to industry, we would shrivel into a meaningless sect. And we must continue to fight within the Fourth International to also make a decisive turn towards this revolutionary current that is extending the Cuban revolution. That is the road toward a real world party of socialist revolution.

The Fourth International was reunified in 1963 on the basis of understanding and embracing the Cuban revolution. It is on this basis, and only on this basis, that we can possibly move forward. There are two ways to turn your back on the workers today. One is not making the turn into industry. The other is not making the turn toward Cuba, Nicaragua, and Grenada and to their revolutionary leaderships.

We will do everything in our power to do what Trotsky advised in the *Transitional Program*, to fight routinism like the plague. We'll do everything in our power to convince every single cadre in the Fourth International to act on their responsibilities, to recognize and respond with enthusiasm to the great new possibilities opened up by the extension of the Cuban revolution. We will fight for that.

And as we carry out that fight, we will speak

unambiguously for ourselves. Our central job—building an American revolutionary workers' party capable of doing the job here—*requires* that.

The interview Maurice Bishop gave Andrew Pulley, Steve Clark, and Diane Wang three weeks ago urged American revolutionists to draw all the conclusions from the fact that only the American working class movement can do "mortal damage to the international capitalist, imperialist system, within the belly of the main imperialist power on earth."

The American working class will act, and will act in time. The American working class will have the same slogan as the Grenadian working class: "Let them come. Let them come. We'll bury them right here."

The American Socialist Workers Party and Young Socialist Alliance say: "Comrades fighting in Guatemala and El Salvador, comrades leading the Sandinista Front in Nicaragua, comrades in our sister party of the New Jewel Movement in Grenada, and comrades of the Communist Party of the Republic of Cuba, without any hesitations or preconditions, we will fight to defend you and we will fight to collaborate with you in building the world party of socialist revolution in every way we can. We are convinced that together we will win."

THE POLITICAL EVOLUTION OF THE CUBAN LEADERSHIP

By Jack Barnes

We've discussed the changes that have occurred within radical Black groups in the Caribbean. The evolution of the New Jewel Movement from Black Power to revolutionary socialism is the most striking example. Black Power groups today are different from what they were in the early 1970s. And under the impact of the Grenadian revolution they have a new potential. There will be new debate and differentiations.

Instead of a nationalist leadership evolving into an obstacle to the development of class consciousness among anti-imperialist nationalists, a class-conscious proletarian leadership has emerged in the NJM that is trying to do the exact opposite. The evolution of the NJM once again confirms that uncompromisingly consistent anti-imperialism leads toward socialist proletarian internationalist conclusions. The example and leadership of the NJM are important not only for the Caribbean, but will also play an important role in the United States. We're just beginning to grasp the impact this development can have here in the United States.

But as Bishop explains, the key to this development is the Cuban revolution and its leadership. It is not the Nicaraguans and not the Grenadians that have evolved the most the last half decade. I think it's the Castro leadership in Cuba. And they are by far the most important factor in the equation. They have the most authority. Their decisions are the most weighty. And they are looked to by revolutionary leaderships developing throughout the region.

I would like to give my opinion on aspects of the evolution of the Castro leadership. We are familiar with the change from the narrowly conceived guerrilla-war strategy of the early 1960s to a much broader, more Leninist-type strategy following the defeats in Latin America. We know about the rethinking that took place in 1968–71, when under the impact of events such as the failure of the "10 million tons" sugar harvest, the Cuban leaders came to grips with what Fidel called their "utopian" period, and made a number of far-reaching changes and adjustments in trade-union policy, economic policy, etc.

But I think even bigger changes have taken place in the last half decade or so. Following the Vietnamese victory over U.S. imperialism, the Cubans correctly understood the change in the world relationship of class forces, and they adjusted their intervention in world politics to take advantage of this. In so doing, they not only further shifted the balance of world class forces and affected the course of history, they also further altered their own thinking.

Think how our consciousness is being altered by the revolutionary changes of the last year and a half. Then use a little imagination about how the Cuban leadership's thinking can evolve as they intervene directly and consciously—with full knowledge of the possible consequences in Washington and Moscow—in such revolutionary events.

The most important single change is the clearer presentation of the perspective of world socialist revolution as the only way forward. Comrades will read the full text of Castro's July 26 speech when *Intercontinental Press* prints it in English in a week or two. Castro's message in that speech is that there is no other road than the road of armed revolution to secure political power and begin the

---

These remarks were made during the discussion on the Grenadian revolution at an expanded meeting of the SWP Political Committee on August 11, 1980, in Oberlin, Ohio. They amplify the final section of the talk "Marxism and the Class Struggle Today."

construction of socialism. He goes over the lessons of Chile, where some tried to do it another way, where they were elected to power and didn't smash the state. He also points to the recent coup in Bolivia to show why the road that Marx called parliamentary cretinism must be rejected.

We know from Bolivian labor leaders that the Cubans urged the small revolutionary groups and leaders of the COB [Bolivian Workers Confederation] to form a labor party based on the COB, as well as COB defense guards to prepare for the coup that would inevitably come. In the struggle against the right-wing and officer caste, they explained the way could be opened for the workers to seize power if they were organized on this powerful basis.

In his July 26 speech, Castro clarifies he is talking about the road every country in Latin America must take. He explicitly includes what he calls the "progressive countries," those whose regimes stand up to imperialist demands that they break trade and diplomatic relations with Cuba. He recognizes, of course, the important role such defiance has played. Yesterday Richard [Fawkes] explained how Cuba's isolation has been partially broken in the Caribbean—this is also true in Central and South America.

Castro demonstratively takes Mexico, Panama, and Jamaica as examples of countries that have stood up to imperialism. He then explains, however, that it is only Grenada, Nicaragua, and Cuba that have done what has to be done. And history demands that every country do likewise.

They have deepened their understanding of differentiations in the semicolonial world. Take the OPEC question, for example. They, like us, begin with the defense of the Arab peoples and the Arab and other oppressed oil producing nations against imperialism. A defense of the right of even the national bourgeoisie to take a larger cut of world surplus value as against imperialism. But their assessment of what needs to be done has evolved over the last few years, along with opportunities to speak out. In some ways, I think they explain what's involved better than we do it.

One of the themes that Castro's been developing in speech after speech deals with OPEC. It's one thing for semicolonial countries with oil to stand up to imperialism, he says, and take a larger cut. That's good. But one of the by-products of this is the role skyrocketing oil prices play in the further devastation of most semicolonial countries. He explains in detail the political economy of how this is done, how it intensifies the imperialist exploitation of the masses of humanity. He explains how this cannot be justified by the fact that the oil-rich semicolonies are confronting imperialism.

For example, in his May Day speech this year in Havana, Castro called on the OPEC nations to come to the aid of the Iranian revolution. "This is OPEC's hour," he said, "the moment of truth for OPEC, when it can show that it is good for something besides raising prices and accumulating big fortunes."

In the speech he gave at the opening of the medical complex in Las Tunas on June 14, Fidel used the example of Venezuela. He asked, what does the Venezuelan regime do with its oil revenues? They don't give much aid to Nicaragua, in spite of all their revenues. They harbor all kinds of counter-revolutionaries in Venezuela, despite their "democratic structure." The audience picked up his train of thought. After he would explain each point about what Venezuela has not done in the anti-imperialist struggle, the audience of 100,000 shouted: "In spite of all their oil revenues!"

The Cubans have developed an entire analysis of the reactionary role of the national bourgeoisies in many of the oil rich semicolonies, and of the obligations these regimes have to the semicolonial countries with fewer resources. They make the differentiation between the exploiters and the exploited not only within every country but on an international scale between countries, just as Lenin did. We support the smaller and poorer against attack or pressure from the bigger and stronger, even if they're both semicolonial countries.

Another point on which the Cuban leadership is speaking out more and more clearly and insistently is proletarian internationalism, the opposite of the Stalinists' "socialism in one country." In his speech to the First Congress of the Cuban CP in 1975, Castro asserted, "According to our Programmatic Platform, Cuba's foreign policy has, as its starting point, the subordination of Cuban positions to the international needs of the struggle for socialism and for the national liberation of the peoples." That this is no ceremonial pronouncement, but instead a guide to action, has been demonstrated from Angola to Nicaragua.

"I am convinced that the world's problems cannot be solved by capitalism or imperialism," Castro said in a speech in March 1977 to Cuban personnel in Luanda, Angola. He then made a moving description of the results of oppression and exploitation he saw on his trip to Africa, and added: "Travelling through all these areas of the underdeveloped world you clearly understand the tragedy of the world and you ask, theoretically, how in the world these problems will ever be solved and how illiteracy, disease, unemployment and poverty will be wiped out. How can human beings create minimal conditions for living with honor, decency, and dignity? How can you do this without revolution? How can you do it without socialism? . . . I say this with more conviction than ever—these problems of humanity have no solution without revolution and socialism. Marx, Engels and Lenin saw these problems very clearly some time ago."

A few days later, speaking to Cuban residents in Moscow, he said, "In Luanda I spoke a long time about this problem of nationalism and internationalism, of the contradictions between the two.

"You can be a socialist yet at the same time develop a national egoism. It's possible. Socialism is the first chance to work for the community, to plan the economy, to help the country and thus to feel a national egoism: all for your own country, and forget the rest of the world."

In the same speech, he analyzed the problems facing humanity, and stated, "It is clear that only socialism can find the answer to these problems—only worldwide socialism, because humanity would have to begin to work as a single family. The more developed countries will have to help the less developed ones—Marx and Engels and Lenin foretold this—as a means toward solving current problems. . . .

"I said that we Cubans are learning to think in a universal way, too. We are acquiring an internationalist spirit. That is the basic conclusion we have reached after observing our people's attitude today. I say that we are learning to be internationalists.

". . . The day will come when no one will doubt that nationalism has to be overcome, too—because, really, what is the nation? A somewhat larger tribe doing much the same thing: the Cuban tribe, the Mexican tribe, the Venezuelan tribe, the Jamaican and Dominican tribes. . . .

"In my view internationalism is the most beautiful essence of Marxism-Leninism. It isn't just a question of being a necessity as the result of a law of evolution of human society. Socialism, internationalism and communism are becoming a necessity for humanity's survival. That is the reality: a condition for humanity's survival!"

In speech after speech, these themes of the need for world socialism, of proletarian internationalism, are developed. A related theme has been the relationship of internationalism to the bureaucratic mentality. In a December 1976 speech to the National Assembly of People's Power, Castro said, "That the most absurd things can happen even within the bosom of the socialist family and in countries that were among the first to take that glorious and revolutionary road, when principles are neglected, when ideas are lost, when men become gods and when internationalism is abandoned, is evident in the recent history of China."

He adds, "And so I think and have always thought that, whatever the individual merits of any man, any evidence of the cult of the personality must be radically avoided; that no man, whatever aptitudes he may be said to have, will ever be superior to the collective capacity; and that group leadership, unlimited respect for the application of criticism and self-criticism, socialist legality, democracy, Party and state discipline and the inviolability of Marxist-Leninist and socialist standards and basic ideas are the only values which can sustain a truly revolutionary leadership."

Raul Castro's speeches last fall against bureaucracy went into this same question.

I don't cite these speeches to argue that there are not errors or ambiguities in them or others. There are. As there are in ours. The point I want to make is that we have to see the Cubans in evolution, as revolutionary leaders who continue to think, learn, and evolve. They are being shaped by what they are doing, what they are learning as they use the power of the Cuban workers' state to help the world revolution.

The current political positions of the Cuban leadership have advanced beyond Che Guevara. If that were not true, they would be nothing but an ossified sect; the whole world has changed in the last thirteen years. And the Cubans have evolved—and grown—along with those objective changes.

One of the persistent myths is that Che Guevara was "better" than, or to the left of, Fidel Castro. That's false. When he was to the left of Fidel Castro, he was wrong. Go back and read *Che Speaks.* Che, for example, limited the necessarily socialist character of the revolution to Latin America, and presented the guerrilla strategy as the only way forward. The Cubans have gone far beyond that. It would lessen Che's historical role to say any different. He explained it movingly in his "Farwell Letter to Fidel."

Cuba and international leadership

The Cubans often express gratitude for the aid they receive from the USSR. They used to concentrate simply on appreciation for the help, without which they could not survive and, of course, this is correct. But new themes have developed in the past few years.

First, they correctly explain what the October revolution meant to humanity. Second, they emphasize that it is the Soviet working people who actually make the aid possible.

There is no change in their praise for the Soviet Union, for the aid they receive, or their explanation of what it means for the Cuban revolution. But they have developed further the idea of the debt the workers of the world owe to the workers whose struggles have brought us to where we are now. This is an integral part of proletarian internationalism, too.

Another theme being developed in Castro's speeches is opposition to "hegemonism." For example, in the July 26 speech he says:

"When I spoke in Revolution Square in Managua I wasn't there to give advice. I said I wasn't there to teach but learn; that I wasn't going to influence anybody, that I was there to be influenced. Any student of history who is really interested in politico-revolutionary processes will learn a great deal from each new revolution.

"There were some people who were worried about Fidel visiting Nicaragua and were wondering if the visit might not be harmful to the Nicaraguans. The Nicaraguans knew full well that I never mentioned visiting Nicaragua and that I never invited myself to go there. They knew full well that I was ready to visit Nicaragua the day and the time that suited them, be it the first year, the second, the third, or the next ten or twenty years, or never. Because we have no use for any vanity, for any kind of chauvinism, or for any kind of hegemonism. Our Revolution wants to be an example; it does not want to be hegemonic. Our Revolution is not interested in appearing as the leader or leading the peoples. We'd be very glad to bring up the rear—the very rear—of a whole revolutionary Latin America and Caribbean. What we're interested in is the revolution, the liberation of our peoples."

I think the Cubans have given a great deal of thought to these questions. They have learned from their own history, from their involvement with the struggles of the Vietnamese, the Africans, and the Nicaraguans, and from giving a lead to the Non-Aligned Movement in the struggle against imperialism. Leadership is not domination. The breakup of the Stalinist monolith, we always insisted, would open the way for revolutionists to take the long, tortuous road back towards Leninism and the Leninist concepts of leadership on a world scale—reknitting the connection with genuine Bolshevism that was almost destroyed by the rise of Stalinism. This is the direction the Cubans are going.

The Cuban army abroad

Comrades remember the public debate, the exchange that we published in *Intercontinental Press* last year, between Alan Jones on one side and David Frankel and Larry Seigle on the other. [See *Revolutionary Cuba Today: The Record of a Discussion,* Education for Socialists, July 1980.]

Alan raised one point in the debate that made us begin thinking more. He argued that if the Cubans were really revolutionists and not centrists, they would have used their "prestige" and "military weight" in Angola to "call for the overthrow of" the capitalist regime. Alan said "there is no doubt" that such a move "would have had every chance of succeeding."

It's clear the Cubans have thought this out to the end too. They understand exactly why revolutions cannot be extended from one country to another on the point of a bayonet. They are conscious Leninists on this.

I read Lenin's debates with Bukharin on this question. Sometimes there can be a tendency to paint an image of Lenin as "tough." Lenin was not tough. He was never tough. He was firm. He was cold-blooded. He was objective. But he was sensitive to the realities of leadership. You can't substitute. You can only inspire and aid those who *can* do the job. The Nicaraguans, the Grenadians had to have a leadership capable of doing the job. The Cubans couldn't do it for them.

The Cuban doctors, teachers, and even troops sent to many countries oppressed by imperialism comport themselves in such a way as to demonstrate that Cuban aid, unlike imperialist "aid," is genuinely without strings, that Cuba is ready to stand shoulder to shoulder with anyone in the battle against imperialism, and its effects, without conditions.

The Cubans obviously know that for their troops to overthrow the Angolan government, or to even be distantly implicated, would be a disaster for the Angolan revolution. And a disaster for the world revolution and for the most important asset the Cubans have, their revolutionary example.

The Cuban army is not the class-struggle leadership of the Angolan toilers. It cannot substitute for them. All it can do is set an example of internationalist aid and show that it will fight in the trenches alongside anyone fighting imperialism.

Think about this question from another angle: their relations with the Grenadians and Nicaraguans. Think about what the Castro leadership could do if it were not proletarian internationalist. The Cubans could abuse their authority and attempt to dominate the revolutionary movements of Grenada and Nicaragua. They could organize factions and try to pick and choose the leadership. Of course they could. Think about the real relationship of forces and the authority they have. They are now faced with something new. And they are showing that they are the opposite of Stalinists in their relations with the revolutionary leaders in Nicaragua and Grenada.

The Cubans' methods provide the sharpest possible contrast to Moscow's intervention in the Afghan revolution and its relationship to the People's Democratic Party leadership in Kabul; invasions, assassinations, and mass purges and jailings are counterrevolutionary methods. Increasingly over the past twenty years, the toilers in Africa and throughout the world have been inspired by and attracted to the example of socialist Cuba. The same can hardly be said about the Kremlin, which has succeeded in Afghanistan in driving growing layers of the population into the hands of anticommunism.

In the December 1976 speech I quoted above, Castro said: "I have always believed that the founders of a socialist revolutionary process acquire such authority, and prestige among their fellow citizens, such far-reaching power, that the unrestricted use of that authority, that prestige and that power can lead to serious errors and incredible abuses."

For the first time, the Cubans are not alone. The revolution has been extended. Now they are challenged to develop correct Leninist relations with the leaders of these new revolutions. And I am confident they are doing and are going to do the right thing to the best of their ability. Others are going to learn from them. This is going to help the Nicaraguans in their relations with the Salvadorans, and so on.

Cuba and the Czechoslovakia invasion

If you go back and read carefully Fidel's speech on Czechoslovakia and Joe [Hansen]'s analysis of it, you discover that the basis on which the Cuban leadership took their stand was their conviction that imperialist intervention in Czechoslovakia had to be stopped. I think that now they see the class struggle more clearly, and how "imperialist intervention" can be used as the final justification of a disastrous course. Their position on Afghanistan would indicate this.

They were also convinced that the internal reforms of the Dubcek regime—concerning the trade unions, the mass organizations, and the structure of the government—were moving away from socialism. They thought the socialist foundations of Czechoslovakia were starting to disintegrate.

But about three years later—after the failure of the 10-million ton sugar harvest and the economic dislocation that created—they carried out a number of "Dubcek reforms" in the economy and trade-union movement.

You can draw one of two conclusions from this. One is that the Castro leadership has been heading to the right over the last ten years, like the Eurocommunists. The other is that they have become more revolutionary, developed a better understanding, from their own experiences, of the relations between collectivization, centralization, democratization, workers' control that is not yet workers' management, etc.

The trade unions have become less simply a mechanism for transmitting party policies into the working class. They have become more of a vital part of the decision-making process. This is the main job of unions in a workers' state—to prepare the working class to govern. As Lenin said, to be schools for communism. The main test of the vitality of the unions is not just how well they protect the workers and solve plant issues. Their ultimate test becomes: is the working class governing more each year, whatever the form?

We can only speculate about what the Cuban position would be in face of a new Czechoslovakia. But if the workers in the foundries and ports of Poland rise up one of these days, as they're preparing to do, and Brezhnev makes the decision to use muscle, whatever the response of the Cubans, I can't imagine it being the same as it was to Czechoslovakia.

I don't know what position they would take, but their refusal to hail the Kremlin's decision to send 100,000 occupation troops into Afghanistan was a break with the Soviet leadership on a major world event. It was even more demonstrative than their dissociation from the Kremlin on Eritrea and El Salvador. The myth that they will always simply praise the intervention of Soviet troops anywhere—not differentiating whether it be counter-revolutionary or an aid to the world revolution—has been destroyed by life.

The point is not to speculate on what they would do with another Czechoslovakia. The point is that their thinking on how the working class can govern has in fact changed. How do you build people's power? What is the role of the trade unions? How do you go from workers' control toward workers' management? How long will this take? How do you go from governing *for* the working class to the *working class governing?* The Cubans are beginning to grapple with this problem, which is the challenge of the historical sweep of the transitional period.

Attitude to Stalinist parties

Someone said in the discussion that there are no Stalinists in Grenada. Well, let me tell you, if there are none, they're coming. This is another problem that is crucially important to the Cubans. How to deal with the CPs?

The July 26 Movement absorbed the Cuban CP, absorbed its best cadres, and removed it as an obstacle. In Nicaragua the same basic process will occur.

The Stalinists are moving in on Grenada. The Canadian Stalinists, for example, are sending a flood of their *Northern Neighbors* magazine. There's more *Northern Neighbors* down there than there are copies of *Intercontinental Press,* the *Militant,* and *Perspectiva Mundial.* They're all over the place.

The Stalinists are everywhere. And they are especially attracted to a situation like Grenada. And the Grenadian leaders are going to have to deal with it just like the Cubans did.

What's happening in El Salvador? The CP is now coming into the political and military coordinating bodies of the revolutionary front, recognizing they were wrong to have initially supported the military-Christian Democrat junta, and recognizing that they have been wrong to reject the socialist character of the revolution. They now say publicly that they were wrong on the progressive role the national bourgeoisie could play in the revolutionary struggle in El Salvador and *elsewhere on this continent.*

The comrades who read Will Reissner's summary in *IP* of the interview with the Salvadorean CP leader that appeared in *Granma* will get its flavor. One of the headlines of the *Granma* was "Late But Not Too Late," referring to the CP's decision to join the armed struggle.

The book *Dynamics of the Cuban Revolution* contains an article by Joe Hansen entitled "How Castro Lost in Venezuela." Joe discussed how their guerrilla strategy disarmed them politically in the fight with the Venezuelan Stalinists. They were politically vulnerable because of the mass work the CPs were involved in. They lost that round in Venezuela.

But something else is happening now. It is the revolutionary current that is winning. In Nicaragua, in El Salvador, in Guatemala, the CPs are being forced to adapt to the revolutionists who say there is no other road—only armed struggle for socialism, to those who see and act on the centrality of the urban proletarian centers, mass work, and construction of a revolutionary party on this basis. This will help the Grenadians to deal with the Stalinists in the right way too.

The same question is going to come up in Bolivia. It looks like the Cubans may finally convince the Bolivians to put together the right kind of front, and the CP is going to have to come into it, for the right reasons.

The Cubans work both with revolutionary currents like the Sandinistas and with the Communist Parties in Latin America. They are part of the world Communist movement. This can be a factor of great importance for the extension of the Cuban revolution.

Practice has clearly demonstrated that the paragraphs of the document of the 1975 Havana Conference of Latin American Communists Parties that could be interpreted as advocating subordination to the national bourgeoisie are not operable. To put it mildly.

A revolutionary Marxist current

There are other points we should study. For example, the Federation of Cuban Women published a book that was originally put out in East Germany called *Men and Women in Intimacy.* It's advertised in *Granma* every week. We haven't seen a copy of it yet, but the *Guardian* recently ran a very favorable review. One chapter is on homosexuality, and it apparently rejects the position that being gay is a sickness.

I don't believe that the publication of this book is accidental. I think it is another indication that the Cubans continue to change and learn.

Their evolution is toward more consistently revolutionary and Marxist positions. Leaderships like the New Jewel Movement and other revolutionary groups emerging in the Caribbean and Central America (and elsewhere too) that look to the Cubans will find an even better Cuban leadership in the 1980s than such movements found in the 60s. Through its experiences, as well through deeper study of Marx, Engels, and Lenin, it has developed a much richer understanding of class politics. It is no less courageous than before, but it is even more Marxist.

Is it correct to call the Cuban leadership Marxist? Are they scientific socialists?

I've changed my mind on this question from what we said last year. The answer seems clearly yes. One thing that started me thinking was rereading Joe Hansen's 1967 introduction to *Che Guevara Speaks,* in which he stated that the Castro team was converging with classical revolutionary Marxism as exemplified by the leaders of the Russian Revolution. That was our commonly held view in 1967 in the SWP and throughout the Fourth International. In 1965 we had referred to the commitment of the Castro-led Cuban Communist Party to "the ideology of revolutionary Marxism." At the reunification congress in 1963 the Fourth International said essentially the same thing. [See Appendix.]

We also tended to refer to the Castro leadership as revolutionists of action. That's accurate. But it sometimes picked up the false accompanying implication that it was something quite different from revolutionists who had well thought out political ideas. Of course, we judge people by their actions. Marxism was developed by Marx and Engels in the course of their participation in the class struggles of the new emerging proletariat. You aren't a materialist if you don't recognize that the best candidates for understanding the theoretical ideas of Marx and Engels are proletarian revolutionists of action.

What's a passive revolutionary, an inactive revolutionary? The action that any revolutionary can engage in may be limited by objective circumstances, but revolutionists who don't act, if there can be such a thing, are certainly not likely to understand Marxism, the theoretical expression of the class interests and struggles of the proletariat. But we began using the term revolutionists of action, as counterposed to Marxist, almost as if we were talking about New Leftists or people like that who reject theory from a petty-bourgeois bias.

I think there is ignorance about the evolution of the Cuban leadership in the Fourth International. I know there was on my part. I stopped carefully reading material from Cuba sometime during the "pause" in the early 1970s. But in that period, as the Cubans grappled with the failure of the guerrilla strategy with what Castro calls their "utopianism" at home, they were not standing still, much less backsliding, in regard to their ideas. Because we weren't following closely what was happening in Cuba we started acting as if it was they who had become silent! But they were evolving and becoming more Marxist on a whole number of questions. They began developing a more Marxist understanding of the oppression of women and the measures necessary to end it. The resolution they adopted on this in 1975 is completely Marxist and parallels our material.

They analyzed imperialism more deeply, and the political economy of the various aspects of imperialist exploitation. They developed their analysis of the semicolonial bourgeoisie and why it cannot liberate the oppressed nations. They began evaluating the role of OPEC. They became *more* convinced that socialism is the only answer.

During this period proletarian struggles in a series of European countries were on the rise. That was the beginning of a general radicalization of the working class in the imperialist countries. And proletarian struggles in the semicolonies began to come to the fore. This deeply affected the Cuban's thinking, too. The growth of the American antiwar movement was followed with close attention by the Cubans, who correctly saw its significance for what was to come within U.S. society.

Looking at all this, we have to say that since 1967, when Joe wrote that the Castro team was converging with classical revolutionary Marxism, this trend has deepened. They are revolutionists of action, yes, and we strive to be too. But they are revolutionists of action whose direction of development for more than twenty years has become more Marxist. Their convergence with Leninism has been increasing, not decreasing.

It is important to see this direction of motion of the Cuban leadership. Our attitude toward them is the opposite of our reaction to a Eurocommunist who tells us that he or she is coming to agree with some of our positions on democracy. We are suspicious of that Eurocommunist. Chances are he or she does not agree with us at all, but is passing us on the way toward the right.

The direction of motion of the Cuban leadership is important in judging their positions. For example, in his July 26 speech, Castro has a section in it about Reagan and the Republican Party platform. He mentions some of the reactionary positions contained in this document, and asks what it would mean for the world if this program were carried out.

"I know that there are some in the United States who would prefer us Cubans not to attack that platform," he says. "They say that owing to certain U.S. public opinion trends to the right, any criticism leveled at that program may help its authors, since we are looked upon as enemies and it might be considered a merit if Cuba should attack that program. Very well, I can understand that point of view. But what's in the cards here is not a U.S. presidential election; what's in the cards may be the fate of humanity, the fate of the world, maybe peace and war.

"That platform must be denounced and world opinion has to be aware of this. It is essential that world opinion react to such a political program. Names are not important to us; we don't care who becomes the president of the United States; we do not intend to get mixed up in that. But we are interested in a situation that derives from the existence of a U.S. party program that threatens the world with war. What is involved here is not just a national but an international question. What is involved here is not just concern for our country but concern for humanity."

Now, this could be interpreted two ways. One way would be to conclude that Castro was playing a subtle trick in order to help Carter and the Democrats get elected. The other way would be to conclude that Castro was dealing with an objective development of some importance and saying exactly what he thought about it, despite unnamed advisors in the United States.

How you interpret such a passage is determined in part by whether you think the Castro leadership is headed in a revolutionary direction or the opposite. This also determines how you present differences with this leadership when they occur, and how you view mistakes it can make. Are they *mistakes,* or are they manifestations of a strategy to the right of revolutionary Marxism?

Our opinion concerning the direction of motion is unambiguous.

Deeper understanding of revolutions

This is not an exercise is scholasticism. We're not interested in labels and abstract categories for their own sake. A small party, and especially one in a country where the working class is only now beginning to move faces an enormous difficulty.

Regardless of your practice, regardless of your involvement in living struggles—and we have never been armchair "Marxists," our party has been built in struggle—you find yourself dealing with the big problems of proletarian revolution as abstractions, as categories.

We took several careful years back in the fifties to decide that China was a workers' state.

In the case of Cuba, we were closer to the revolution. We had China and Yugoslavia behind us. More of us knew its history, language, culture, and people. So we didn't take as long. But even in this case, our convention decision on Cuba in 1961, which confirmed what our National Committee plenum had decided earlier in 1961, was retroactive—looking back on a process that had occurred.

In the case of Nicaragua, because of this experience, we were even more prepared. We moved more quickly, and have been able to intervene as the process itself has developed.

But it's not just learning to move faster. The pace of world politics has also accelerated. And most importantly, we've learned more about the problems of revolution.

One of my educations the last couple months has been reading a book called *Anarchism and Anarcho-Syndicalism*, with selected writings by Marx, Engels, and Lenin. [Progress Publishers, Moscow.] It contains all the basic writings of Marx and Engels on the struggle against anarchism, ending up with the fight with Bakunin. It includes a series of articles about the Spanish revolution of 1873–74, in which Marx and Engels deal with the question of how communists should relate to a revolutionary provisional government. Lenin picks up this subject, quoting Marx and Engels extensively, around 1905. [See pages 187–202 in the collection.] Later, right on the eve of the 1917 revolution, he returns to it.

These are the kinds of questions we are trying to grapple with. It's not a matter of simply pinning labels like workers' and farmers' governments or workers' state on a revolutionary process at some given moment. What Lenin, Marx, and Engels were dealing with was the question of *intervening* in the revolutionary process. I thought for almost twenty years—if I gave it any thought at all—that it would have been wrong for a revolutionary Marxist to accept a post in the Cuban government between January and September of 1959. Maybe other comrades had a different view. But not many. But I always thought that this was a bourgeois coalition government in a bourgeois state, and this precluded participation. Thus it would have been a fundamental break with Marxism to have participated in such a government.

Joe always argued that the attack on Pablo for accepting a post in the Ben Bella government before it became a workers' and farmers' government was wrong. Pablo's error was that he acted as if he had a mass base when he didn't; and he failed to work with other revolutionists in Algeria to build a Marxist tendency, gathering together Leninist cadres, against the right wing of the FLN. But far from being wrong, his participation in the government could have and should have facilitated doing this. His participation in the government was real. It was based on the respect that the Algerian revolutionists had for Pablo and for our world movement. Our comrades did courageous things in Europe during the Algerian war. They saved the lives of many Algerian fighters, carried out many important assignments, and they had a good reputation in Algeria when the French were defeated.

The Leninist position is not that Marxists should not serve in a government issuing from a revolution unless it is what we would call a workers' and farmers' government.

What is a provisional revolutionary government? It is a provisional government that arises out of a revolution. Such a government often includes representatives of all the forces that come together in the revolutionary overthrow. It can include a majority of bourgeois figures, like the original Cuban government did. And as in Cuba, a provisional revolutionary government can—as the revolution deepens and the balance of class forces shifts—be transformed into a workers' and farmers' government. This process always involves a series of confrontations and tests of strength with the bourgeois and vacillating petty bourgeois forces. And only with a certain high caliber of leadership and a favorable evolution of the relationship of class forces based on a deep mass mobilization does this transformation become possible.

The question I'm addressing is different from

whether a workers' and farmers' government could have been set up in Cuba from the beginning, as happened in Nicaragua. Perhaps it could have, had the July 26 leadership been as Marxist then as it is today. But in some revolutionary overthrows, the relationship of class forces might prevent that from happening at the outset. Whether or not to take a post in such a government is a tactical question. How long to keep a post in such a government is also a tactical question. You might resign after the first week. You might be offered the post of minister of labor, come in with five proposals to strengthen the organization and arming of the working class, not be able to carry out your program, and demonstratively resign, explaining the truth to the workers and using it to mobilize them in struggle.

The goal of whatever tactics employed regarding such a government is to advance the revolution. In Cuba, wouldn't refusal to join the revolutionary government have been tantamount to giving the leadership to the bourgeoisie? Refusal to join the government would have meant the failure to use *every* means at the Cuban toilers' disposal—inside and outside the provisional government—to bring the power of the workers and peasants to bear to safeguard the revolution and drive it forward. It would have meant simply turning over the entire power and authority of the government emanating from the Cuban revolution to the class enemy—before even testing whether the masses and their independent organizations and mobilizations could alter the balance of forces to their favor and bring into being a regime based on the workers and peasants.

Finding labels for the government does not solve every tactical problem. How do we mobilize and educate our class to carry through the seizure of power and consolidate a government based on the revolutionary masses?

Cuba and the Kremlin

Finally, it's my opinion that the Cuban leadership is heading for more open conflict with the Soviet bureaucracy. I think it has already begun. I think Brezhnev is unhappy about what is happening in Central America. I do not think this is in the interests of the Soviet bureaucracy. In addition, I think the Cubans may be on their own if they use troops in Latin America outside the borders of Cuba to combat imperialist aggression.

Any idea that there is a strategic identity of interests between Havana and Moscow is dead wrong. Of course, compromises will have to be made, and we do not know how the differences in policy between the Soviet bureaucracy and the Cuban leadership will be expressed. It will be settled behind closed doors for as long as possible.

But as the socialist revolution initiated by Cuba continues to extend and Washington does whatever it can to counter this, as the influence of the Cubans grows, including in the CPs in Latin America, the Soviet bureaucracy will have greater and greater misgivings. If that is not true, we would have to conclude that the Kremlin is going through a process of self-reform. On the contrary, what the Soviet bureaucracy appears to be searching for is a deal with the new administration in Washington following the elections.

EXCERPTS FROM DOCUMENTS OF 1963 REUNIFICATION CONGRESS

A convergence in assessment of the Cuban revolution was among the major political factors that made possible the reunification of the world Trotskyist movement in 1963. The Fourth International had been divided for a decade into two organizations.

At the June 1963 Reunification Congress, delegates discussed the importance of the Cuban revolution and the emergence of the Castro leadership team for resolving the worldwide crisis of working-class leadership. Below are passages from two resolutions adopted at that Congress.

The first is from "Dynamics of World Revolution Today"; the second is from "The Sino-Soviet Conflict and the Situation in the USSR and the Other Workers States."[1]

The victory in Cuba marked the beginning of a new epoch in the history of the world revolution; for, aside from the Soviet Union, this is the first workers state established outside the bounds of the Stalinist apparatus. Such a development, whatever the size of the country involved, was a turning point whose effects have necessarily reverberated on a tremendous scale throughout the whole world Communist movement.

In fact an international Castroist current has appeared inside the world Communist and revolutionary-socialist movement which, as was to be expected, is strongest in the colonial areas, especially Latin America and Africa. It is also noticeable in the other workers states. In Algeria the influence of Castroism again testifies to the importance of the Cuban development.

Except in Spain and Portugal, Castroism has not had great impact in Europe. Its influence in other metropolitan centers such as the United States and Japan is likewise limited. One of the reasons for this is that the Cuban leadership has not yet reached an understanding of how it can best facilitate revolutionary rebirth in these areas.

The appearance of more workers states through further development of the colonial revolution, particularly in countries like Algeria, would help strengthen and enrich the international current of Castroism, give it longer range perspectives and help bring it closer to understanding the necessity for a new revolutionary Marxist international of mass parties. Fulfillment of this historic possibility depends in part on the role which the Fourth International plays in the colonial revolution and the capacity of sections of the Fourth International to help win fresh victories.

The infusion of Trotskyist concepts in this new Castroist current will also influence the development of a conscious revolutionary leadership, particularly in the workers states, will help prevent "Titoist" deviations and better assure the evolution of mass pressure and direct action into the cleansing force of political revolution. The development of the Portuguese and Spanish revolutions, historically possible in a short period, can also give rise to new tendencies of the Castroist type which would help the Cubans and related currents to achieve a fuller understanding of the process of world revolution in its entirety.

THE FIDELISTA CURRENT

In the present context of the Communist movement, a completely specific place is occupied by the Fidelista leadership which will more and more

1. The first resolution was printed in *Dynamics of World Revolution Today* (New York: Pathfinder, 1974). The second, "The Sino-Soviet Conflict and the Situation in the USSR and the Other Workers States," appeared in *Fourth International* no. 17, October–December 1963.

play a genuinely international role, above all, of course, in Latin America. This leadership is distinguished from other leaderships of the workers states not only from the point of view of its origins but also in relation to its positions on international and internal problems.

If some of its members individually reached Marxist positions before participating in the July 26 Movement, the Cuban leadership as such had no precise theoretical formation and it expressed, even up to the taking of power, confused and equivocal ideological concepts. But, thanks, to profound links with the masses, especially with the most disinherited layers of Cuban society, it was more and more able to understand the genuine logic of the revolutionary process and, despite its ideological limitations, it worked in practice along a line of permanent revolution, assuring the creation of the first workers state in the Americas. Thus Cuba became the first example in our epoch of a revoluion in which the leadership through its own experiences in the very course of struggle came over to the concepts of Marxism-Leninism.

Subsequent experience has proved that this is a profound conversion. In brief,

(*a*) The Cuban leadership is the first leadership of a workers state since Lenin and Trotsky that has addressed the exploited masses—on a continental scale—to call them to revolutionary struggle for the conquest of power. (See the Second Declaration of Havana.)

(*b*) Through their speeches and declarations, Fidel Castro and his comrades have shown that they envisage the problems of the Latin-American revolution under an essentially revolutionary angle, rejecting the Khrushchevist concepts of the majority of the Latin-American Communists. The speech of Fidel Castro to the Congress of American Women (January 1963) marked another decisive step forward on this level.

(*c*) Nationally, the Fidelista leadership, keenly sensing the bureaucratic dangers which were threatening and can still threaten the Revolution, intervened in conscious fashion, as the Left Opposition sought to do in the USSR and in the Bolshevik party, in order to appeal openly to the masses to struggle against bureaucratization and to assure a series of concrete organizational measures (following the elimination of Escalante).

Thus, the Fidelista leadership appears at this stage as the most advanced political leadership by far of all the workers states. Even if it engages only very discreetly in the current international debates, due to the fact that while its revolutionary line is without doubt closer to the Chinese line[2] it requires Soviet economic and military aid, still it will be in a position to exercise growing international influence, above all in Latin America, but also in other colonial and semicolonial countries and even among the youth of the capitalist countries and the workers states.

---

2. The Reunification Congress took place at an early stage in the Sino-Soviet conflict, when the Peking bureaucracy was leveling a series of public attacks on Moscow's open bid for a deal with U.S. imperialism. To sweeten the pot in this bid, the Kremlin had cut off needed military and economic aid to Peking at a time when China still faced unrelenting Cold War hostility and military pressure from Washington. The Fourth International utilized this debate and the criticisms from the left then voiced by Peking to raise the revolutionary Marxist alternative to the Stalinist conceptions of "socialism in one country" and "peaceful coexistence" with imperialism.

EXPAND YOUR REVOLUTIONARY LIBRARY

Labor, Nature, and the Evolution of Humanity

The Long View of History

FREDERICK ENGELS, KARL MARX
GEORGE NOVACK
MARY-ALICE WATERS

Without understanding that social labor, transforming nature, has driven humanity's evolution for millions of years, working people are unable to see beyond the capitalist epoch of class exploitation that warps all human relations, ideas, and values. Only the revolutionary conquest of state power by the working class can open the door to a world free of capitalist exploitation, degradation of nature, subjugation of women, racism, and war. A world built on human solidarity. A socialist world. $12. Also in Spanish and French.

Women's Liberation and the African Freedom Struggle

THOMAS SANKARA

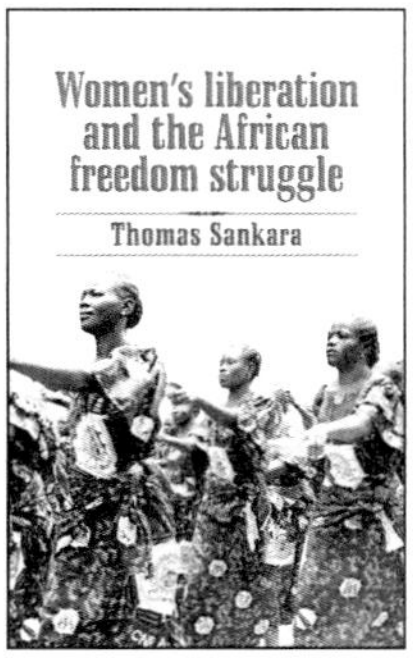

"There is no true social revolution without the liberation of women," explains the leader of the 1983–87 revolution in the West African country of Burkina Faso. $5. Also in Spanish, French, and Farsi.

Women in Cuba: The Making of a Revolution within the Revolution

VILMA ESPÍN, ASELA DE LOS SANTOS, YOLANDA FERRER

The integration of women in the ranks and leadership of the Cuban Revolution was intertwined with the proletarian course of the leadership of the revolution from the start. This is the story of that revolution and how it transformed the women and men who made it. $17. Also in Spanish, Farsi, and Greek.

50 Years of Covert Operations in the US

Washington's Political Police and the American Working Class

LARRY SEIGLE, FARRELL DOBBS
STEVE CLARK

How class-conscious workers have fought against the drive to build the "national security" state essential to maintaining capitalist rule. $10. Also in Spanish and Farsi.

The Low Point of Labor Resistance Is Behind Us

The Socialist Workers Party Looks Forward

JACK BARNES, MARY-ALICE WATERS
STEVE CLARK

The global order imposed by victors of the inter-imperialist slaughter of World War II is shattering, with explosive ramifications for workers and farmers worldwide. A long retreat by the working class and unions has come to an end. More and more workers of all ages, skin colors, and both sexes are saying, "Enough is enough!" This book highlights opportunities ahead for class-conscious workers to forge a labor party built on the unions. And a mass proletarian vanguard able to lead the struggle to end capitalist rule, opening a future for humanity. $10. Also in Spanish and French.

By Any Means Necessary

MALCOLM X

"The imperialists know the only way you will voluntarily turn to the fox is to show you a wolf." In eleven speeches and interviews, Malcolm X presents a revolutionary alternative to this reformist trap, taking up political alliances, women's rights, US intervention in the Congo and Vietnam, capitalism and socialism, and more. $15

The Rise and Fall of the Nicaraguan Revolution

Based on ten years of socialist journalism from inside Nicaragua, this special issue of *New International* recounts the achievements and worldwide impact of the 1979 Nicaraguan revolution. It traces the political retreat of the Sandinista National Liberation Front leadership that led to the downfall of the workers and farmers government in the closing years of the 1980s. Documents of the Socialist Workers Party by Jack Barnes, Steve Clark, and Larry Seigle. In *New International* no. 9. $14. Also in Spanish.

The Communist Manifesto

KARL MARX AND FREDERICK ENGELS

Communism, say the founding leaders of the revolutionary workers movement, is not a set of ideas or preconceived "principles" but workers' line of march to power, springing from a "movement going on under our very eyes." $5. Also in Spanish, French, Farsi, and Arabic.

Capitalism and the Transformation of Africa

Reports from Equatorial Guinea

MARY-ALICE WATERS
MARTÍN KOPPEL

Describes how, as Equatorial Guinea is pulled into the world market, both a capitalist class and a working class are being born. Also documents the work of volunteer Cuban health-care workers there—an expression of the living example of Cuba's socialist revolution. $10. Also in Spanish and Farsi.

The History of the Russian Revolution

LEON TROTSKY

How, under Lenin's leadership, the Bolshevik Party led millions of workers and farmers to overthrow the state power of the landlords and capitalists in 1917 and bring to power a government that advanced their class interests at home and worldwide. Unabridged, 3 vols. in one. Written by one of the central leaders of that socialist revolution. $30. Also in French and Russian.

Maurice Bishop Speaks

The Grenada Revolution and Its Overthrow, 1979–83

The triumph of the 1979 revolution in the Caribbean island of Grenada under the leadership of Maurice Bishop gave hope to millions throughout the Americas. Invaluable lessons from the workers and farmers government destroyed by a Stalinist-led counterrevolution in 1983. $20

Democracy and Revolution

GEORGE NOVACK

The limitations and advances of various forms of democracy in class society, from its roots in ancient Greece through its rise and decline under capitalism. Discusses the emergence of Bonapartism, military dictatorship, and fascism, and how democracy will be advanced under a workers and farmers regime. $17

To See the Dawn

Baku, 1920—First Congress of the Peoples of the East

How can peasants and workers in the colonial world achieve freedom from imperialist exploitation? By what means can working people overcome divisions incited by their national ruling classes and act together for their common class interests? These questions were addressed by 2,000 delegates to the 1920 Congress of the Peoples of the East. $17

Cosmetics, Fashions, and the Exploitation of Women

JOSEPH HANSEN, EVELYN REED
MARY-ALICE WATERS

How big business reinforces women's second-class status and uses it to rake in profits. Where does women's oppression come from? How has the entry of millions of women into the workforce strengthened the battle for emancipation, still to be won? $12. Also in Spanish, Farsi, and Greek.

Dynamics of the Cuban Revolution

A Marxist Appreciation

JOSEPH HANSEN

How did the Cuban Revolution unfold? Why is it an "unbearable challenge" to US imperialism? Why are its lessons important to working people everywhere?

In "Cuba—The acid test: A reply to ultraleft sectarians," one of more than 20 articles here, Hansen starts with facts—not doctrine pretending to be theory—to examine the class struggle unfolding in Cuba in the 1960s. He refutes the political blindness of leftists who denied the dialectical richness of the socialist revolution and communist leadership developing before their eyes.$23

America's Revolutionary Heritage

Marxist Essays

GEORGE NOVACK

$23

The Revolution Betrayed

What Is the Soviet Union and Where Is It Going?

LEON TROTSKY

In 1917 workers and peasants of Russia were the motor force for one of the deepest revolutions in history. Yet within ten years a political counterrevolution by a privileged social layer, whose chief spokesperson was Joseph Stalin, was being consolidated. The classic study of the Soviet workers state and its degeneration. $17. Also in Spanish, Farsi, and Greek.

Are They Rich Because They're Smart?

Class, Privilege, and Learning under Capitalism

JACK BARNES

In battles forced on us by the capitalists, workers will begin to transform our attitudes toward life, work, and each other. We'll discover our worth, denied by the rulers and upper middle classes who insist they're rich because they're smart. We'll learn in struggle what we're capable of becoming. $10. Also in Spanish, French, Farsi, and Arabic.

Teamster Rebellion

FARRELL DOBBS

The 1934 strikes that won union recognition for truckers and warehouse workers in Minneapolis and helped pave the way for the working-class social movement that built the industrial unions. The first of four volumes by a central leader of these battles. $16. Also in Spanish, French, Farsi, and Greek

The Jewish Question

A Marxist Interpretation

ABRAM LEON

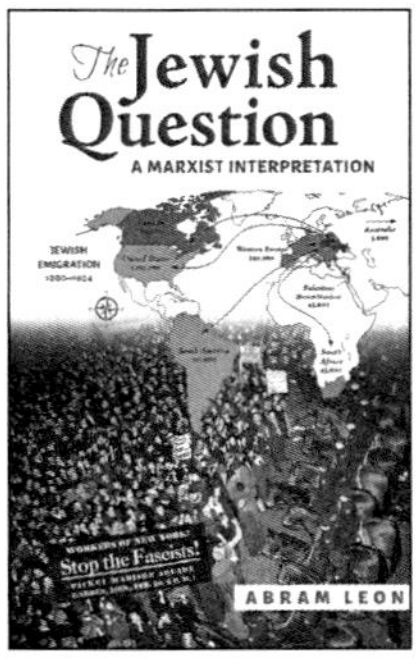

Why is Jew-hatred still raising its ugly head? What are its class roots—from antiquity through feudalism, to capitalism's rise and current crises? Why is there no solution under capitalism? The author, Abram Leon, was killed in the Nazi gas chambers. Revised translation, new introduction, and 40 pages of illustrations and maps. $17. Also in Spanish and French.

Che Guevara, Cuba, and the Road to Socialism

ARTICLES BY ERNESTO CHE GUEVARA
CARLOS RAFAEL RODRÍGUEZ
CARLOS TABLADA
MARY-ALICE WATERS
STEVE CLARK, JACK BARNES

Exchanges from the opening years of the Cuban Revolution and today on the political perspectives defended by Guevara as he helped lead working people to advance the transformation of economic and social relations in Cuba. In *New International* no. 8. $14. Also in Spanish.

We Are Heirs of the World's Revolutions

Speeches from the Burkina Faso Revolution, 1983–87

THOMAS SANKARA

How peasants and workers in this West African country established a popular revolutionary government and began to fight hunger, illiteracy, and economic backwardness imposed by imperialist domination. They set an example not only for workers and small farmers in Africa, but their class brothers and sisters the world over. $10. Also in Spanish, French, and Farsi.

Pathfinder Press **accessible ebooks** for the blind, those with low vision, or other challenges reading print books

For a list of current accessible titles, go to: pathfinderpress.com/collections/books-for-the-blind.

Visit bookshare.org for information on how to sign up.

THE CUBAN REVOLUTION AND WORLD POLITICS

October 1962

The 'Missile' Crisis as Seen from Cuba

TOMÁS DIEZ ACOSTA

In October 1962 Washington pushed the world to the edge of nuclear war. Here the full story of that historic moment is told from the perspective of the Cuban people, whose determination to defend their sovereignty and their socialist revolution blocked US plans for a devastating military assault. $17

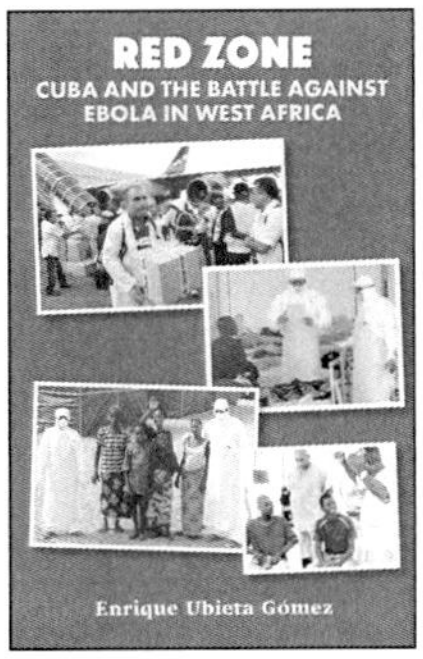

Red Zone

Cuba and the Battle against Ebola in West Africa

ENRIQUE UBIETA GÓMEZ

When three African countries were hit in 2014–15 by the Ebola epidemic, Cuba's revolutionary government sent what no other country even pretended to provide: more than 250 volunteer doctors, nurses, and other medical workers. This firsthand account of their actions shows the kind of men and women only a socialist revolution can produce. $17. Also in Spanish and French.

The First and Second Declarations of Havana

Nowhere are the questions of revolutionary strategy that today confront men and women on the front lines of struggles in the Americas addressed with greater truthfulness and clarity than in these uncompromising indictments of imperialist plunder and "the exploitation of man by man." Adopted by million-strong assemblies of the Cuban people in 1960 and 1962. $10. Also in Spanish, French, Farsi, Arabic, and Greek.

The Inevitable Battle

From the Bay of Pigs to Playa Girón

JUAN CARLOS RODRÍGUEZ

The rout of US-organized and -financed forces at Girón Beach on Cuba's Bay of Pigs in April 1961 was Washington's greatest military defeat in the Americas. It has marked the course of history for the last sixty years. $20. Also in Spanish.

Our History Is Still Being Written

The Story of Three Chinese Cuban Generals in the Cuban Revolution

ARMANDO CHOY, GUSTAVO CHUI
MOISÉS SÍO WONG
MARY-ALICE WATERS

"What was the key measure to uproot discrimination against Chinese and blacks in Cuba? It was the socialist revolution itself." New edition sheds light on Chinese Cubans' involvement in Cuba's internationalist course, including in Africa and Latin America. $15. Also in Spanish, French, Farsi, Greek, and Chinese.

Cuba and Angola: The War for Freedom

HARRY VILLEGAS ("POMBO")

The story of Cuba's unparalleled contribution to the fight to free Africa from the scourge of apartheid. And how, in the doing, Cuba's socialist revolution was strengthened. $10. Also in Spanish, Farsi, and Greek.

Cuba and the Coming American Revolution

JACK BARNES

This is a book about the struggles of working people in the imperialist heartland, the youth attracted to them, and the example set by the Cuban people that revolution is not only necessary—it can be made. It is about the class struggle in the US, where the revolutionary capacities of workers and farmers are today as utterly discounted by the ruling powers as were those of the Cuban toilers. And just as wrongly. $10. Also in Spanish, French, and Farsi.

Che Guevara Talks to Young People

Guevara challenges the youth of Cuba and the world to work. To become disciplined. To join the vanguard on the front lines of struggles, small and large. To become a different kind of human being as they fight together with working people of all lands to transform the world. $12. Also in Spanish and Greek.

RELATED READING

Lenin's Final Fight

Speeches and Writings, 1922–23

V.I. LENIN

In 1922 and 1923, V.I. Lenin, central leader of the world's first socialist revolution, waged what was to be his last political battle—one that was lost following his death. At stake was whether that revolution, and the international communist movement it led, would remain on the revolutionary proletarian course that brought workers and peasants to power in October 1917. $17. Also in Spanish, Farsi, and Greek.

The Struggle for a Proletarian Party

JAMES P. CANNON

"The workers of America have power enough to topple the structure of capitalism at home and to lift the whole world with them when they rise," Cannon asserts. On the eve of World War II, a founder of the communist movement in the US and leader of the Communist International in Lenin's time defends the program and party-building norms of Bolshevism. $20. Also in Spanish and Farsi.

In Defense of Marxism

Against the Petty-Bourgeois Opposition in the Socialist Workers Party

LEON TROTSKY

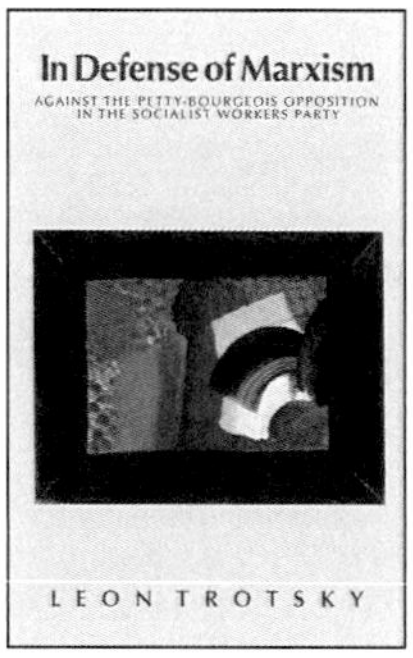

A reply to those in the revolutionary workers movement in the late 1930s bending to bourgeois patriotism during Washington's buildup to enter World War II. Trotsky explains why only a party fighting to bring workers into its ranks and leadership can steer a communist course. In the process, he defends the materialist and dialectical foundations of Marxism. $17. Also in Spanish.

The History of American Trotskyism, 1928–38

Report of a Participant

JAMES P. CANNON

$17. Also in Spanish and French.

The Transitional Program for Socialist Revolution

LEON TROTSKY

The Socialist Workers Party program, drafted by Trotsky in 1938, still guides the SWP and communists the world over. The party "uncompromisingly gives battle to all political groupings tied to the apron strings of the bourgeoisie. Its task—the abolition of capitalism's domination. Its aim—socialism. Its method—the proletarian revolution." $17. Also in Farsi.

Socialism on Trial

Testimony at Minneapolis Sedition Trial

JAMES P. CANNON

The revolutionary program of the working class, presented in response to frame-up charges of "seditious conspiracy" in 1941, on the eve of US entry into World War II. The defendants were leaders of the Minneapolis labor movement and the Socialist Workers Party. $15. Also in Spanish, French, and Farsi.

Their Trotsky and Ours

JACK BARNES

To lead the working class in a successful revolution, a mass proletarian party is needed whose cadres, well beforehand, have absorbed a world communist program, are proletarian in life and work, derive deep satisfaction from doing politics, and have forged a leadership with an acute sense of what to do next. This book is about building such a party. $12. Also in Spanish, French, and Farsi.

The Challenge of the Left Opposition

LEON TROTSKY

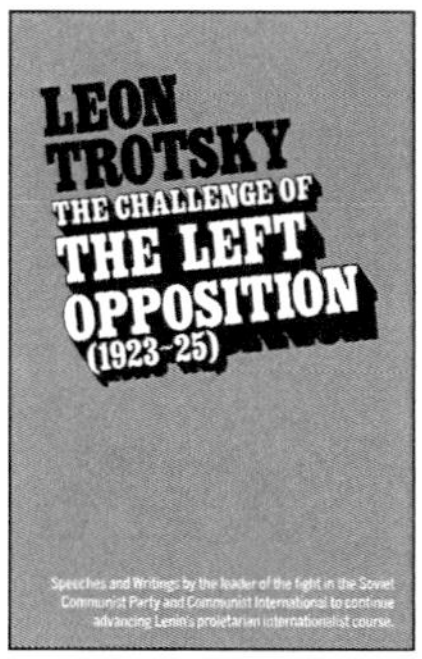

This three-volume series documents the fight of the communist opposition from 1923 to 1929 against the reactionary political and economic policies of the rising bureaucratic caste in the Soviet Union. Vol. 1: 1923–25, $25; vol. 2: 1926–27, $25; vol. 3: 1928–29, $25.